SPOTIFY PROFITS 2.0

MUSIC MARKETING AND BUSINESS STRATEGIES FOR THE NEW SINGLES ECONOMY

CHRIS GREENWOOD

ABOUT THE AUTHOR

Chris Greenwood, aka Manafest, is a barrier-breaking singer, songwriter, rapper, and author with over 1,000,000 monthly listeners. He effortlessly merges rock, rap, and pop throughout his music, carefully assembling experiences and compelling inspirations that speak to a wide variety of fans across the globe.

His unique style has garnered notable achievements, such as four JUNO nominations, multiple GMA Dove nominations, and a slew of GMA Canada Covenant Awards. His music has been featured in the NFL, video games, throughout television shows such as *Knight Rider, One Tree Hill, MTV Unplugged*, and most recently in the movie *Hard Target 2*. His intelligent and contagious music has sold over 300,000 albums worldwide, and Chris has performed over 1,000 shows across four continents.

CONTENTS

Chapter 1:
WHY SPOTIFY?

Dear artists, musicians, songwriters and music creatives

The battle between streaming versus selling physical or digital albums has finally been won, and I'm happy about the winner. I truly believe that Spotify is the best thing that has ever happened to artists and musicians in the 21st century.

Like all innovations that change the way we do things and shake up the norm, it's a platform that isn't without its critics, and maybe you've found yourself getting caught up on the much-debated issue of the lower royalty rate per stream. If so, I invite you to take your focus away from that detail and look at what Spotify gives you: the opportunity to get your music heard by millions of people around the world, and to get paid every time they listen to your songs — whether they're a one-time listener or whether they play your songs every day.

Personally, I think that beats the old model where a fan bought your CD and you'd only get paid once. Now, that same fan can listen to their favorite song of yours for decades to come and you'll receive royalties for every one of those streams.

This has changed how we share our music in a phenomenal way. We no longer have to get fans to buy our music, but what we have to do instead is encourage them to listen. And that's what this book is all about.

I've been mastering Spotify since 2012, and at the time of writing I've just hit 130 million streams. That blows my mind, and I'm beyond grateful.

I've had months where I've made more money in Spotify royalties than what I was paid in a year — maybe several years — during my time as a signed artist with a label. When I look inside my Spotify Artist dashboard and see fans are streaming my music in countries I've never even heard of, I get excited. I love the fact that Spotify shows me real live data of how many fans are currently listening to my music. Just the other day I saw that 700 people were listening all at one time, which was awesome to see. Have you ever performed to 700 people in a packed club before? It's quite the experience, yet that's happening virtually every day on Spotify, with listeners all around the world connecting via our music.

So welcome to the jungle of the online music business! I think we need to give the creators and co-founders of Spotify, Daniel Ek and Martin Lorentzon, a round of applause for creating such an amazing platform for artists. In this business, distribution is king and Spotify has allowed us, the artists, to make our music available to fans at the touch of a screen or the click of a button. No more having to sign away our master rights or publishing rights to record labels just so we can sit at the table of success. Now all are welcome.

With that being said, we do need to acknowledge that there's an increase in competition. Now anyone can release a song, good or great, and with over 60,000 new songs uploaded daily to Spotify, our main question as artists, and the question I will endeavor to answer in these pages, is now this:

How do we get our music heard in such a crowded music marketplace?

If you already know me, or have read any of my previous books or attended any of my courses, you'll know that sharing information like this is a passion of mine.

I started out as a total underdog: I failed music in school (I like to think God has a sense of humor) and was probably one of the worst rappers and singers you ever heard, but I was willing to surround myself with artists and producers that were better than me. I took mental notes and applied every skill I could learn to my songwriting and performances. Even when I signed to a record label, I always stayed independently-minded because I knew I was the architect of my own destiny. And you, my friend, are the architect of yours.

If you keep doing the same thing over and over again but your fanbase is not growing, then something has to change. Most of the time I tell artists just because something is hard doesn't mean we're going the wrong way. It just means we might need a new strategy. To evolve, it's important that we don't get too attached to our way of thinking or doing things. The more I learn and grow in the music business, or any business, the more I realize how much I actually don't know.

If we are not growing then we are falling behind. That means if Spotify's customer base is growing by 10% year over year and your fanbase isn't — then we've got a problem.

"We've got to be willing to be bad at something long enough until we get good at it."
— Myron Golden

I've been touring and recording music since 2000, and in 2005 I quit my job to pursue music full time, which means my career has grown in tandem with the seismic changes that have occurred in how we listen to, consume, and share music.

As well as those 130 million Spotify streams, I've grown my followers to over 1 56,000, and when I first started using the strategies I'm sharing in this book, I finally hit one million monthly listeners in the space of a couple of years.

Something everyone wants to know, and something I'm keen to be transparent about is this: How much can you actually make from Spotify streams?

Let me share some numbers to give you an idea. One of my newer songs just hit 1,043,477 streams and that earned me $3,185.75 in royalties from my distributor.

That works out to about 0.003 cents per stream, which a lot of artists might look down their noses at — but hold on a second.

I look at songs as investments or assets that earn me money every day.

That song has now been out a year and still gets 5,000 streams a day, which works out to about $15 a day in royalties. That's $450 a month, and $5400 a year, in passive income.

Now that may or may not seem like a lot of money to you, but what if you had ten or twenty songs generating that amount of royalties?

That's where it gets exciting.

And that isn't even my most popular song, and the numbers and profits I'm sharing here are just from Spotify, not including any of the other streaming platforms I use to share my music.

But just do the Spotify math: twenty songs generating $5400 a year each in passive income gets you an annual sum of $108,000. That's what I call Spotify Profits!

That level of income takes time, and tenacity, and a willingness to keep working at your dream. On these pages I'll share every ninja secret I have up my sleeve to help you. Let's get you to the place where you're living your dream and making the money you want to make as a successful artist killing it on Spotify.

Welcome to the future: your future.

Embracing the Singles Economy

> *"Sometimes it only takes one song to bring back a thousand memories."*

That quote above is a well-known sentiment that you often hear from people who are passionate about music, and who know the power of a single song. Songs can represent a moment in time and an entire lifetime all at once. They're powerful and they're in demand, now more than ever before. And while I'm not going to declare that the album as an art form is dead (how can it be when vinyl sales continue to rise?) there is no doubt that we have moved into a singles economy, where fans want to cherry-pick and listen to the songs that they resonate with, without having to buy a whole album just to access them.

There are some major advantages for us as artists in this new landscape. We can try out new ideas and get our music out there faster without having to spend money on a full album with all the related recording and marketing costs. Another plus is that we don't have to commit to one producer or songwriter for a whole album, but instead can collaborate with different creatives for different songs.

It's worth noting here that it is actually pretty dangerous to hire one producer for a whole album, especially when you've never worked with them before on a song. Think of it like this: it's best to date before you get married. I've heard too many horror stories of artists committing to a full album or EP with a producer only to be disappointed with the final product. Why not pick the best song out of the handful you've written, and commit to recording that song with a producer to see not only if you work well together, but if you can produce a hit song together.

Going back to the singles economy, what I love the most about the emphasis on songs over albums is that it allows artists to focus on one song at a time. That way they can not only make a song the greatest it can be, but they also get to pay attention to how they market it and promote it.

Then, they can move to the next song, riding on the momentum they've built, and keep going, song by song, until they're ready to release an album — which by now will be packed with hit songs (I recommend around eight singles for a ten-song album) that have already reached and touched a huge number of listeners. There's more coming on this method of releasing songs in Chapter Three. I call it the Spotify Waterfall Release Strategy and it's an awesome way to get the most out of the singles economy.

So, that's where we are, and this is the music industry as it is today. I have to say I get excited by all of this because we have so many more opportunities to connect, reach and delight our fans than we've ever had before. It's just a case of doing all we can to get heard.

So let's dive into it!

Chapter 2:
INSIDE YOUR ARTIST PROFILE

"Focus on the possibilities for success, not the potential for failure." — Napoleon Hill

As we go along, it's going to be useful if you have a Spotify account set up and that you've claimed your artist profile. If you haven't already, head to artists.spotify.com or download the 'Spotify for Artists' app on your preferred device. There are plenty of online resources and guides with whichever service you distribute your music through that will take you through the technical aspects of setting up an account and using the features I'm talking about here, so I don't want to take time and space in this book with that kind of detail. Instead, everything I point you towards or advise you to do is based on increasing your reach, touching more people with your music, and getting those all-important followers, streams and royalties.

In this chapter we're going to look at some of the ways you can customize your Spotify artist profile so your fans' first impression of you is in line with who you are as an artist.

Let's take a brief look at some of your options.

Your banner image

The banner image, which runs across the top of your profile, does two things: it sets the mood for your page, and it gives you the opportunity to lightly promote whatever you'd like to draw your listeners' attention to. Note that term I'm using here: lightly promote. Spotify actually state in their guidelines for artist images that you can't include text or promote upcoming releases. I once tried promoting a Crowdfunding campaign by sharing my website on my banner image and Spotify asked me to change it.

But what you can do is feature the associated artwork from your new single or album on your banner. Whatever you choose, remember it's the first thing fans see when they visit, so make it count. Go for an image you feel reflects your brand, your style, your music. It's always cool to change your banner image from time to time, especially with a new single release. It keeps things fresh and regular fans will appreciate it.

If you have issues getting the right dimensions for your banner (2660 X 1140), Canva.com provides free online image editing software. I use it for this and many other social media design tasks and it's great.

The image gallery

Aside from being able to choose your banner and a profile picture, Spotify also gives you the space to upload multiple photos in your image gallery, giving you a chance to show your fans even more of a flavor of who you are. I suggest getting creative and sharing a variety of images here, including a great press photo, shots from any live shows you've done, plus any other images that will please your current fans and allow new ones to get to know you. Anything that reflects your brand and your music is good because fans aren't just following you for your music, they're following you for your style and what you stand for. You can update your biography here as well; I like to include a call to action, usually directing people to my website where they can sign up for my email list.

Concerts

If you're touring or doing live shows you can link to any upcoming performances on the 'concerts' tab within your profile, as long as the shows are listed with a ticket partnering site like Songkick or Ticketmaster. If I was still touring I would be taking advantage of this feature for sure! I'd also be running ads on Spotify to promote tours and shows, something we'll be exploring later in the book.

Merch

Inside your artist profile there is a tab called 'Merch' which allows you to connect your Shopify store to your Spotify profile. This is an incredible update that literally allows you to showcase merchandise from your online Shopify store for fans to purchase. They currently allow you to spotlight three merch items, and even if you don't have physical merchandise you can connect your Shopify store to a print-on-demand service like **Printful**, who handle all printing and shipping for you.

More info

Under the 'more info' tab you can point your fans to your social media pages like Instagram, Twitter and Facebook, and also your Wikipedia page if you have one. To be honest, I don't love my Wikipedia page so I just leave that blank. One thing that's missing here but would be useful is the option to link to your website, but the workaround here is to mention it in your bio.

Artist Pick

The Artist Pick feature allows you to control the music that appears at the top of your artist profile and currently, in beta test mode, you can even showcase merchandise here. You can use your Artist Pick to feature any song or album on Spotify, a playlist of your choice, or, as I just mentioned, a merchandise item from your Shopify store. At the time of writing, I'm using my Artist Pick to promote my latest album. Looking around I see Linkin Park are promoting a playlist of their best songs, Justin Timberlake is linking to a playlist called his 'Top tracks', while Fall Out Boy are promoting a playlist featuring all the bands they're currently on tour with. That's a pretty smart move because the description of the playlist encourages fans to go and buy tickets.

When choosing what you want to have as your Artist Pick, have an image in mind that can go with it, whether that's a press photo, or a cover image from an album or single.

Keep in mind that whatever you choose for your Artist Pick it only lasts fourteen days, so keep updating it and keeping it fresh or else it will expire. One way to do this is to reach out to another band or artist you know and offer to promote their songs in your Artist Pick for a week. This works both ways — part of the deal is they link to your tracks, too. This costs you nothing but an email or a social media message, and it's a great way to boost each other up. My advice is to always look at other artists as your collaborators, not your competition. There's more on that coming later in the book.

Adding a canvas to your songs

A canvas is a 3-8 second visual loop you can create that plays vertically, filling the screen, when someone is listening to one of your songs. Each song gets its own canvas, so you can give each track its own vibe and character. This is an awesome opportunity to showcase moving artwork, or a clip of your music video to listeners, or whatever visual you feel suits the music. I'm certain that people have gone on to check me out on YouTube after seeing a clip of a music video in a canvas on Spotify.

There's good evidence to show that canvases are working well for artists. According to a Digital Music News article, a high-quality Spotify canvas video can improve the performance of your song. One stat said Spotify canvas increased shares by 145% and playlist adds by 20%. The article also said 9% of fans are more likely to visit your profile and you can expect a 5% increase in streams.

It's worth noting that the current requirements for Spotify canvas is 3-8 seconds in length for videos, vertical 9:16 ratio, and between 720px – 1080px tall. Plus the file has to be either in MP4 or JPG file.

Canvases are an awesome way to engage with your fans, so I urge you to get creative and explore this very cool feature. Two places you can easily create a Spotify canvas for free are Canva.com, which allows you to upload and edit your own videos. The other place I recommend is Distrokid, which actually supplies free video clips and allows you to easily edit them.

Chapter 3

THE WATERFALL RELEASE STRATEGY FOR SPOTIFY

"Just because your music is free doesn't mean you don't still have to sell it."– Manafest

Next up we're looking at what I consider to be the best method for releasing your songs on Spotify, a method that will maximize your exposure and create a buzz and awareness around your music. It's time to look at what I call The Waterfall Release Strategy, where you release multiple singles leading up to a full-length album or EP release.

In the days before Spotify and similar platforms, artists would release between one and three songs from an album before launching it. As I said in the previous chapter, my advice, to really make the most of the singles economy and increase your streams and chances of getting added to Spotify editorial playlists, is to release around eight songs from an album before launching it (based on a 9-10 song album).

Albums don't sell albums; singles sell albums. Think about it: if you have a favorite album it's not because of the album itself but because of the song or songs that were on that album that emotionally touched you. And now, with Spotify, we have more chances to connect and inspire our fans than ever before.

The two key aspects of the Waterfall Strategy are consistency: you need to be releasing a new song every 6-8 weeks; and great marketing in between: each song should have a proper campaign behind it to ensure success.

This takes a certain level of organization, patience, and creativity — plus a willingness to plan ahead.

> ### *"A goal without a plan is just a wish."*
> ### *— Antoine de Saint-Exupéry*

If there is one thing I learnt from being in the label system it's that they were organized when it came to release dates and setting up timelines for going to radio, organizing tour dates, shooting videos and so on. When a signed artist doesn't turn in a record on time the release gets pushed back, because the label knows they can't just rush things out or they're not going to make the money back on the record. It's that simple.

And now, even as the masters of our own success, I still see so many independent artists rushing to get their songs out without paying proper attention to the marketing.

The truth is, if you're just releasing songs — even using the 6-8 week schedule I'm suggesting here — without promoting or marketing each one in between the releases, you are not going to grow your fanbase nearly as fast as you could. Every song you release deserves its own promotional campaign. If you want more help with that I suggest you read my book **Music Marketing & Promotions Guide** for ideas or join our next Spotify challenge at 10xyourfanbase.com/livechallenge.

Patience pays

I know how exciting it is to finish a song in the studio, get it mastered the next night, and want to share it with the world the very next day. But doing this hurts the song's chances of success in numerous ways — and it's not just the opportunity to have a proper launch campaign that we miss out on.

When you rush a release out you also forfeit getting on Spotify's Release Radar, which notifies all your followers and the algorithm playlists of new releases. The Release Radar requires seven days notice if you want to be included.

You also forgo the opportunity to get on an editorial playlist, because to be considered for a playlist you need to submit your unreleased track 1-2 weeks before its release date. Those much-coveted editorial playlists are put together by Spotify's curators who are experts in their genre, and they have the power to bring you thousands and thousands of streams — which could lead to thousands and thousands of new followers. There's more advice coming up later in the book on the specifics of pitching your songs to Spotify's playlist editors, plus more information on what the Release Radar can do for you.

For now, let me show you how I used the Waterfall Release Method on my album, I Run with Wolves.

Waterfall in flow

In the months leading up to the album release date, we released seven songs as singles, and those singles came out every other month, accompanied by either a music video or a lyric video.

By the time the album dropped, five of those seven singles had gotten onto editorial playlists. Sometimes it was *Hard Rock, Core, New Music Friday* or another playlist in the metal genre. It's good to note that it takes time for Spotify to get enough data to categorize you as an artist and switching genres constantly does NOT help you. This comes back to the power of focus. Pitching your song inside your artist's dashboard also triggers the Release Radar to ensure all your followers are notified. I promoted each song hard after its release so that my fanbase grew in between each song. I'll be sharing ideas on how to promote your songs throughout the book, and particularly in Chapter Six where we look at how to grow a genuine fanbase.

Then, when we released the album, we pitched a song called *Break the Habit* which also got onto six different editorial playlists. To date that song has 475,000 streams after being out three months. It's important to note that out of the 475,000 streams, 252,000 of them came from exposure on editorial playlists — so they really do make a huge difference.

Plus almost every song that I released I made new artwork for. I'm a firm believer in the notion that *fans don't hear you first, they see you first.* My wife Melanie helps me and dozens of other artists craft artwork for their single and album campaign launches. Contact her at Visioncityart.com.

It's interesting to note here that there are only two tracks on that album which have tens of thousands of streams rather than hundreds of thousands like all the others. What's the difference? Those two songs weren't released as singles. They weren't pitched to the Spotify curator team, and the Release Radar was also not triggered. We are talking about 80% less streams. That's the power of planning.

	I Run With Wolves		11,302,136
	Album		
	Only 2 songs below 100,000 were NOT singles		
1	Dead Man	⟶	62,678
2	I Run With Wolves		916,531
3	Forever		283,134
4	UPS AND DOWNS		796,568
5	Gravity Falls		345,303
6	Nemesis		1,059,679
7	Break The Habit		636,969
8	Brain Dead		276,168
9	Save You		3,231,412
10	Doomsday	⟶	60,586
11	Blackout		706,467
12	Light It Up		2,926,641

If I could go back in time I would have held back at least one of those songs and released it on its own as a single, and then maybe included it as part of a deluxe version of the whole album. Another thing I could have done is kept it on the CD version but held it back from the digital. That way I could motivate fans who want that song now to buy the CD. What frustrates me is that each song cost me just as much in time and money to write, record and release, but those two won't recoup nearly as fast because they weren't properly released and promoted.

The truth is, even artists with thousands of followers will get very few streams if they rush the uploading process.

Going forward, to really make the most out of the Waterfall Release Strategy I suggest you lead with your best songs, and don't hold anything back. Your first single release should be your strongest song.

Once a song has been released, Spotify's algorithm kicks in notifying all your followers, and for a good 4-6 weeks you'll see the streams coming in. They'll slowly start to taper off by week four, depending on how much external marketing you're doing, how big your following is, and whether you got accepted onto an editorial playlist and triggered the Release Radar.

In my experience, if a song isn't connecting in a big way with listeners after its release, I'll see the number of streams slowly starting to reduce, and then the number of streams will average out at hundreds or thousands of listens a day.

Other times the song does not taper off at all and in fact gains momentum because Spotify's algorithm has picked it up and shared it via all their algorithmic playlists. This is always the best scenario.

After about six weeks it's time to release another song to give Spotify's algorithm another boost and notify all your fans about your new music. And so your streams shoot back up again, and once again, after 4-6 weeks the streams will start to tether off, so that's when you want to release your next song. If you're just starting out, you'll notice that as you release your second or third song all your songs will get a lift in streams with each new song you put out, because fans will be checking out your back catalog.

We will touch on this later in the book, but there should be marketing outside of Spotify to continue to push the song, like promoting to indie playlists, running ads, and even getting social influencers on board. Every song released should be launched to a growing audience of fans, not just the same ones.

Just like a waterfall, your single releases cascade, there's a consistent flow, and, if you'll forgive a little cheesy pun here: they make a splash!

I really hope you can embrace this as a new method of reaching fans and making the most of what we can do with Spotify. There's a ton more to discover but I just wanted you to get the basics of how to release your songs before we dive deeper.

Chapter 4:
EDITORIAL PLAYLISTS: IN DEPTH

It's time now to take a look how you can get your songs included on a Spotify editorial playlist. These are the playlists curated by Spotify's music experts, and they can be based around a genre, a sub-genre, or even a mood or a vibe. It's easy to see why getting a spot on a editorial playlist is a big deal for a lot of artists: they have the power to put you in front of millions of new listeners, increasing your streams and your reach by 10X.

Before we get into it, I just want note that you cannot buy on to a Spotify editorial playlist. You can only pitch your song to be considered, and that's a process which is 100% free. In fact anyone offering to add your song to their playlist in exchange for money is against Spotify's terms of service. So let's look at how you can give your song the best chance of being included in an editorial playlist.

The pitching process

First up, as we looked at in the previous chapter, it's essential to give Spotify and their editorial team 1-2 weeks to listen to your song before its release date, but personally I'd go further here and encourage you to give them even more time by submitting your song at least a month ahead. These guys have thousands of songs to listen to and consider, so that extra time is only going to go in your favor. You don't want to be known as the guy always being late or down to the wire.

The other thing you want to be aware of is when you submit your song via your artists.spotify.com dashboard you'll be asked to go through the song pitching process. This involves answering questions about the song, its genre, and other contextual information such as the cultural influences and the mood. In essence, you're describing your song so it gets in front of the right curators for your style of music, so do pay attention to this.

Steve Shirley, a senior product manager at Spotify, points out that, "You're in this sea of more than 2000 songs that come in [to the curators] every single day." He goes on to talk about how being thorough with the information you give when you pitch will increase the chances of getting on a playlist, adding, "We're not saying it's a requirement ... but it definitely increases your chances."

It might sound obvious but make sure you answer the questions honestly; if your song is a hip-hop song don't pitch it for indie rock or country. I've noticed the more I stay focused by releasing in one genre of music and not jumping from different styles, the better success rate I have with getting on editorial playlists.

The next thing you want to consider is the information you write in the pitch box.

I believe the strongest part of your pitch should be having a great song, but there are other ways you can stand out. When it comes to the pitch box, my advice is to lay everything out that you're going to do to market the song. This should include a full marketing plan with your budget for ads, details about the music video or lyric video, any publicity you'll drum up, any touring you have planned, accolades you already have, plus TV/Film placements that would make your song stand out from the rest of the songs that get pitched.

That's the key here: stand out. Do all you can. With that in mind, I always thank the curators in my pitch. So many industry folks are treated poorly and are never appreciated — so stand out by being kind.

The extra mile

Here's something else you can do to stand out: get familiar not only with the playlists that feature your genre of music, but also the employees at Spotify who run that genre. For instance, there's a head of rock music, a head of country, a head of hip hop — a head of almost every genre. It's true that a lot of these jobs have been replaced by Spotify's algorithm, but there will always be tastemakers at the top of each genre who influence the big playlists.

Having a good relationship with a Spotify curator in your genre of music can pay dividends for years to come. It's great if they can put a face with your name and your music, because whether we like it or not, when it comes to business a lot of success comes from who you know — so make yourself known.

I've done this myself, and it works. I took the time to research the head curator of my genre of music at Spotify, and I sent packages through the mail as well as emails, all to introduce myself and make myself known. Taking the time and effort to establish a relationship in this way has resulted in my songs getting included in more editorial playlists than if I had remained a stranger, so I strongly suggest you adopt this approach too. As Grant Cardone says, "If they don't know you, they can't flow you."

Do your own research via Google and LinkedIn to begin with, and get the names of the person or people who look after your genre. If you notice they're speaking at any music conferences, go along if you can. At the very least, follow them on social media.

As I'm sure you'll appreciate, anyone in a powerful music marketing position, whether it's at Spotify, Amazon, Apple Music or within a music label, will be getting hit up by artists begging for their attention on a daily basis. Most artists contact these people the wrong way, say the wrong thing, and wonder why nobody ever responds or gives them the time of day.

That's why I developed what I call the *Knock Knock Method* for my coaching students, and I'm about to share it with you here. It's basically a step-by-step guide on how to build a relationship with someone in the industry, making you and your music stand out from the other thousands of artists begging for their attention.

The *Knock Knock Method* requires strategy and planning, and you need to have a long-term plan in mind. That begins with deciding what your goal is in contacting this person. For this book we're going to stay focused on Spotify, so our goal is to get your song added to a Spotify playlist. Here's what I suggest you do.

The Knock Knock Method for Spotify

Step #1: Find out who the head of your genre is at Spotify.

Step #2: Follow them on social media (wherever they are most active).

Step #3: Start commenting on their posts and show your support by sharing their posts too — but DO NOT ask for anything.

Step #4: After a week, DM them thanking them for what they do for artists.

Step #5: A few days later, DM them something short and sweet like this: *Hey, Love what you're doing! My name is Manafest, I'm a rock* *artist from Toronto and just released a new song. I'd love for you to check it out!* Then insert the link to your song on Spotify.

Step #6: Mail them a package. Because you've been following them for a couple weeks, maybe you've noticed they like chocolate, or Starbucks, or a certain type of food. Mail them a package to their office with a handwritten note thanking them and asking them to check out your song. NOT album, song! Stay focused.

Step #7: Follow up every other week with emails, DMs, and two more packages — even phone calls.

How do you feel reading that?

I want to share a hard truth with you here: Step 7 is where 99% of artists give up. Why? It could be that they're overwhelmed, it could be because they don't want success bad enough.

Here's my advice:

Be willing to do what 99% of what most artists won't do, so you can have what 99% of artists will never have.

I have a million monthly listeners because I was willing to do this stuff. Most record labels won't even go to these lengths to put you and your music out there.

If this seems like too much, take a minute and think about what you actually want here. Success? Streams? Fans all over the world hearing and connecting with your music?

Then you know what you need to do. Knock knock! You got this.

Chapter 5:
ALGORITHMIC PLAYLISTS: IN DEPTH

"Release Radar alone generates more streams than any of Spotify's self-curated playlists." – Bryan Johnson, Spotify UK Director of Artists & Management

As awesome as it is to get included on an editorial playlist, they do kind of steal the show in conversations around getting your songs out there. While they carry a lot of prestige, I have to be straight-up honest here: in my experience, it's the algorithmic playlists that generate the most streams for me, yet they are the least talked about in most artist circles. Maybe they have a sense of mystery around them, or they're not well enough understood. Or maybe some people are a little snobby about the algorithm! Who knows. The key is these playlists can bring in hundreds of thousands of streams, so understanding how they work can only be a good thing.

Let's start by looking at two of the most important algorithmic playlists on Spotify: Discover Weekly and Release Radar.

Both of these playlists are uniquely created for each user, with Discover Weekly being made up of songs Spotify thinks a user might enjoy based on the genres and artists they already listen to; and Release Radar featuring new music releases by artists that a user already follows or has shown an interest in.

Unlike editorial playlists, algorithmic playlists do not require any human intervention; they're automatically compiled based on each user's individual listening habits. Even if you're not a regular Spotify user, I'm sure you've noticed something similar to this yourself with TV streaming services like Netflix; they recommend certain movies or TV shows based on what you've watched already.

Spotify, just like the TV streaming services and other companies like Facebook and Google, are investing millions in their AI (artificial intelligence) technology to gather data about their users so they can match the right songs with the right fans. Spotify is constantly collecting behavioral data from listeners based on the songs they listen to and the way they listen to them.

Before I go on, I just want to say that I'm not writing this book to argue for or against the moral issues around privacy and data collection. What's important for us here and now is to know that Spotify is collecting that data all the same, and using it so its AI can know who to recommend our songs too. I'm looking at it as a benefit rather than a breach on privacy.

As a marketer of my music I like the fact it targets fans based on their interests. This is powerful, and a good investment of my money. In fact, a couple of days ago I checked my stats on YouTube and saw this beautiful comment under one of my music videos: *"Spotify said I would like this, and it was right."*

That's the power of Spotify's algorithm in action. Not only did this new fan listen to my song on Spotify, but they were motivated enough to go to YouTube, a different streaming platform, and watch the music video I had created. I love that!

Furthermore, I've heard through the musical grapevine that Spotify is going to be switching to more machine learning for deciding which songs get added to playlists. Don't quote me on it, but if true, this could be a huge opportunity for lesser-known artists because if your song is doing well then it can be automatically added to a playlist without you having to do a thing.

Everyone wants to land a big editorial playlist when their song first comes out, and while this is a great goal, the fact is you can get dropped from such a playlist sometimes a week or a few weeks later. Sure, I've had some that have kept me on much longer, but it's important to note the algorithmic playlists, once triggered, can bring you streams for months on end.

With all that in mind, let's take a closer look at what kind of data Spotify is collecting to create these algorithmic playlists.

Some of the data Spotify tracks

Among other things, Spotify is interested in the length of the songs users listen to, when they pause them, if they search for something else mid-listen, if they skip a song, add it to a playlist, save the song, or share it on social media.

Skip rate on a song can be a particularly brutal statistic for us as artists, because if a song has a high skip rate, and if it keeps happening, then Spotify is going to stop recommending that song and possibly remove the song from playlists. Remember Spotify wants to give their users the best experience, so it's nothing personal. That's why sometimes you might get a shot on a big editorial playlist, but you don't last long on there because your song has a high skip rate.

On the other hand, the gathering of this data can work for us in a positive sense because if a song has a low skip rate that means fans are listening to a track the whole way through, and then Spotify knows to share it to more of its users. My song, *Stones*, had been on some of the bigger playlists and stayed on there over a year because it had such a low skip rate.

The other positive data Spotify tracks is if fans are saving or hearting the song, and if they're sharing it to social media. This could also include embedding it on their website or blog. Spotify can also track where fans are coming from, especially if they are new customers.

Spotify — obviously — wants new customers to come to their site, so if you're leading them there with your music then extra kudos for you. This is another reason why promoting your songs is really essential, something we'll dive into later in the book.

Spotify Radio and Your Daily Mix

Before we move on, I just want to give you a heads up on two other powerful playlists which are good to know about along with Discover Weekly and Release Radar. These are Spotify Radio and Your Daily Mix.

I'm sure by now you're understanding that Spotify believes a user's listening experience should be very personalized; both of these newer playlists serve that mission.

Spotify Radio is a feature which creates a collection of songs based on any artist, album, playlist, or song of your choice. It even updates over time to keep your playlist fresh. However, it's worth noting that Spotify Radio offers less of a chance for listeners to discover new music, this is more of way for them to listen to what they already know and love. With the advent of Spotify Discovery Mode now new fans can discover your music via this new recommendation tool inside of Spotify's AI.

Your Daily Mix, on the other hand, is a playlist that will throw in some new music in amongst what it knows a user already likes.

Each user has up to six Daily Mix playlists available to them, and these playlists are updated daily, to keep fans listening non stop.

I actually like listening to my Daily Mix, I see it as my own personal DJ playing my favorites, and injecting a few new tunes by artists I might not have heard before.

Next up I want to tell you about a cool feature called **Spotify Discovery Mode**. Discovery Mode gives artists the opportunity to influence Spotify's personalization algorithm in two locations where listeners discover new music: Spotify Radio, which we just covered, and Autoplay playlists. When Discovery mode is turned on for a song, it increases the likelihood but does NOT guarantee a song will reach listeners in Radio and Autoplay. Artists choose to turn Discovery Mode on or off for any track in their catalogue that is eligible.

After personally turning on Spotify Discovery Mode for a campaign for my songs I saw 109,385 new listeners from radio and autoplay, a 268% listener lift (which is my daily average monthly listeners during the campaign), and, my favorite stat to share: 27,695 new listeners who had never streamed my music prior.

Some of the other impacts were 985 saves during the campaign and 708 playlist ads.

Spotify Discovery requires no up front cost, giving artists at any stage of their career a chance to participate. However, there is a 30% commission on recording royalties generated from all streams of that song from Radio and Autoplay. All other streams that take place after outside of Radio and Autoplay remain commission-free which I think is freaking awesome. Where do I sign up?

It's also important to note I said recording royalties are only required to pay a commission, not publishing royalties, for a chance to get a 268% listener lift.

But before you get too excited, not every track is eligible for Spotify Discovery Mode.

Here are the eligibility requirements which should become your goal for every one of your songs.

#1 Your song must be distributed with a DSP (Digital Service Provider) like TuneCore or DistroKid

#2 The track has to have been released on Spotify for at least 30 days

#3 The track must have been streamed in Radio or Autoplay in the last seven days

Reach out to your distributor with any questions about this, as Spotify Discovery Mode has just finished up its beta test pilot.

To wrap this chapter up, I just want to say that I hope you're getting how powerful these playlists are. If you've got a hit song and it gets tons of plays, then Spotify's algorithm will pick it up and begin to share it via their algorithmic playlists, and a domino effect sets in. When your music gets shared automatically like this, it's amazing. With every share and bunch of new fans reached, there's the potential for your song to reach even more.

Of course, we don't just release a song and hope for the best. There's way more we can do as independent artists to steer our ship, reach more fans and keep the algorithm working for us — and that's what we'll explore next.

Chapter 6:
BUILDING, AND GROWING, A GENUINE FANBASE

"Money can't buy me love." — The Beatles

If you use social media you've probably heard about bots: those automated profiles that can share, like, follow, even send messages, and yet there's no 'real' person at the end of these accounts. There are companies out there who sell bot activity to social media users who want to increase their numbers, and these companies also target Spotify artists, by offering thousands of streams in exchange for what's usually a pretty small sum, say around $50. And if you were to find yourself weighing up this option, you might think it's worth it at first, after all $50 is way less than you'd spend on advertising. And the process is instant — unlike taking the time to genuinely reach and connect with people who you hope will become your fans.

But please, do not fall for an offer like this! You may get your streams, but you won't keep them. As soon as Spotify picks up on it, they'll remove them.

Spotify say: *"An artificial stream is a stream that doesn't reflect genuine user listening intent, including any instance of attempting to manipulate Spotify by using automated processes (bots or scripts)."*

Spotify are all about the user experience, they want genuine user listens — and so do we.

In short: you can't buy a fanbase, you have to earn it.

And when you think about it, do you want thousands of fake streams? Or do you want real people listening to your music and being impacted by what you penned and recorded?

I write songs for real people. I don't want pretend fans, and neither does Spotify, because it messes with the algorithm. As we've explored, Spotify's algorithm is designed to collect data based on real users' listening habits so it can recommend our songs to more people. Your goal should be to find genuine fans, get added to real users' playlists, and become known to real people who listen to your music and can become part of your fanbase.

So that's what this chapter is all about. Later in the book we'll look at how we can purchase advertising to get our songs genuine impressions, but right now we're looking at mostly cost-free approaches you can take to get genuine listens, build a community, and keep that community coming back for more.

The thing is, being a successful artist has always required hard work, and you could argue that's required now more than ever. The simple truth is there will always be more talented artists out there than you and I, and some of those artists' songs and music will never see the light of day. Yet others who are less talented than we are will be killing it — and you won't be able to figure out why.

But if there's one thing I've learned, it's that you can't be a recluse in this industry. You can't just release music and hope and pray for a big label or a great manager to discover you, save you and bring you to your dreams. You have to get out there and do it yourself — and this focus and drive is something that many of those less-talented yet super-successful artists have.

Not only are they willing to write songs and promote them, but they put themselves out there and build something worth more than a 7-figure record deal.

It's called *community*.

Super-successful artists know who their fans are, and they post every day and talk to them as friends, and as equals. They might even have a name for their tribe. Their appreciation for their fans is clear, and they build such a tight-knit bond that this community becomes the birthing place of their super fans: those incredible people who show up to every concert, buy every piece of merch, and support every crowdfunding campaign you do.

I am so blessed to have my own tribe. I call them my Fighters! Their support, belief and enjoyment in what I do and stand for is a huge motivator for me. I strongly suggest you interact with your fans on social media, be interested in what your supporters have to say, ask questions, get their input, and be kind! It costs nothing. Your fans will notice it, appreciate it, and they'll keep showing up for you, however they can.

And in turn, you show up for them by not only giving them awesome music, but getting creative with merch, getting personal on socials, being consistent, and being generous.

Let's look at each of these areas in turn.

Getting creative with merch

"What gets promoted gets played." — Manafest

Creating merchandise around your single launch is a strategy I want you to be thinking about for every song you release. Don't just make an awesome, timeless song and throw it out into the wild hoping that something will happen. Start thinking about creating individual marketing campaigns for each song you put out there using the Waterfall Release Strategy we looked at in Chapter Three.

When I release a song, we create artwork around it. We design t-shirts and other merchandise inspired by the single cover. This allows us to make additional income from the song — not just off of the streams. We created an awesome T-shirt for the last song I released and we made hundreds of dollars off of it before we even released the song. That T-shirt continues to be a best seller.

Have fun with this, and if you don't do design yourself check out VisionCityart.com, where you can hire   a freelance designer who specializes in music artwork to create designs that are right for your brand. I've said it before and I'll say it again: my wife Melanie is awesome at this. Look her up at visioncityart.com.

Getting personal on socials

It goes without saying that you need to be making cool and interesting music videos for each song you release, and you should make your videos available on your YouTube channel plus any social media you use. I also suggest you make lyric videos too, and going further, why not record short videos where you chat about the song, what it means to you, and why you wrote it? Think of these like 'behind the scenes' mini movies.

They can be super short and you don't need a fancy location. In fact, fans like to see you chilled and in a natural environment. Be engaging and passionate when you talk about your music, or whatever you want to share about your creative process. Your fans will love this. Think about the bands and artists you love, do they share glimpses behind the curtain so you can understand more about them? If they don't, how much would you dig it if they did?

I encourage my students to find their own unique voice and angle, so they're expressing themselves online not just about music, but also whatever else they stand for or are passionate about. Maybe that's fashion, fitness, politics or a social justice issue. Or maybe for some people it is all about music, and if that's the case keep it fresh by covering all the different areas, like your songwriting process, the music gear you use, how you shoot your videos, or the ups and downs of touring.

The point I'm trying to make is that you can build a massive tribe, not just around your music — but around YOU. Then your fans will support whatever you do, whether it's music related or not. Create and share your own unique story. Fans want the original, exclusive YOU that only you can be, they don't want an annoying echo of someone else.

Instagram stories is a great tool for connecting and getting personal with your fans. Use it to promote your songs and keep your music in front of people. As well as the mini movies we just talked about, you can post clips of your older songs and share them in seconds. If you have a back catalog, go back and grab something that you haven't posted in a while, especially if an anniversary is coming up of an album or a song you haven't posted about in a long time. Say something like, *Hey guys, remember this song?* and add a little spoken or written anecdote if you want to, perhaps sharing what memories it brings back for you.

Something else to keep in mind is this: just because you've posted a song once on Instagram doesn't mean you can't post it again. I re-post songs over and over again because people are busy, plus they need to be reminded of me over and over again! Just because I have 32,000 followers on Instagram doesn't mean they all saw the story or post the first time around. I'm going to need to post it again, to keep my music in my fans' ears, and my brand on their mind.

If you don't have a big catalog, no worries — just keep releasing new music and continue to build it up.

Something that's pretty cool is that anyone can include a link in an Instagram story now, so I suggest you use this feature with a call to action. As we're talking about Spotify here, link to your Spotify playlist that's made up of a catalog of your songs.

In short, you want to be promoting the junk out of anything you release, because you want to drive as much traffic to Spotify as possible. More fans equals more traffic, which equals more streams, which equals more chances of getting on algorithmic playlists, which means more exposure, which means more fans... you get the picture!

Being consistent

As we looked at in Chapter Three, I recommend releasing a song every 6-8 weeks to really take advantage of the singles economy and to keep your name and your music out there. This is how you give your fans something fresh while triggering Spotify's algorithm.

Before I get into this section, the thing I really want you to realize here is that I'm not saying whip out a whole bunch of half-baked songs just to keep releasing something every six weeks! Please do not do that. It's better if you release one smash song in a six-month period than five mediocre tracks. One hit single can do more for your career long term than three full, but uninspired, albums.

So consistent *and* high-quality releases are essential if we're going to keep building our fanbase, and keep our fans happy. Having said that, I know that for some artists the 6-8 week schedule can be a big ask, especially when factoring in the costs of recording in the studio, mixing and mastering, plus outsourcing the artwork, designing merch and any other marketing costs.

With this in mind, one strategy I utilize myself is to create new songs on a smaller budget by repurposing an already existing song from my back catalogue. I might do a remix, or an acoustic version, or release the instrumental version of the song — or even a full album of instrumentals. This way you can continue to pump out great new content without breaking the bank. This is also a great opportunity to get another artist to feature on a song, something we'll discuss later on in the book.

Repurposing older material is great for attracting new fans and it's satisfying for your current ones. Sometimes fans will miss a song release but when they're there on your page on Spotify, they'll notice it, check it out, and maybe play others they just haven't heard for a while. And then the algorithm kicks in, notices a lot of people are playing your music or saving your new song, and, as we know — there's a good chance that peak in streams will help get you added to an algorithmic playlist. Win win!

Being generous

"No one has ever become poor by giving." — Anne Frank

Have you ever had someone give you an unexpected gift at Christmas, or perhaps at another time of year, totally out of the blue? A gift that really surprised you. Besides feeling thankful, and appreciating how thoughtful the person was, I bet you also had a sense that you'd like to give back to this person in some way.

This is why I recommend giving music away to your fans. It should also be noted here that you should never give away a song that you couldn't sell for a profit. What do I mean? If it's not good enough to sell then why would you dare try to give it away for free, thinking it would build a fanbase or even make a good impression to new fans? Don't rush the process! Make good music first before trying to market it, even when you're giving it away for free.

Not convinced about the giving-it-away-for-free thing? Hear me out!

When we give our music away, we invoke the law of reciprocity, which means those who have been touched by our music will want to give back. Sure, not all of them, but a lot of them. And getting your music out there to as many people as possible, even if that means giving it away for free, is how we initiate the process.

The following little anecdote demonstrates the power of the law of reciprocity in action. I remember walking past a Panda Express in the mall and being offered some of their orange chicken. After just one piece I was sold! I wasn't even planning on eating there, but they got me with the free sample. They were giving away their best-selling item for free, and I was so grateful and inspired that's where I went for lunch.

So, how do we give our music away to our fans?

There are two ways I recommend. One is to use something called a download gate, which is essentially where we ask for something from a fan — it might be something as simple as an email address, a follow on Spotify, or to pre-save our upcoming song, and in turn we give them a free download of that song. Pretty simple. I use a service called Hypeddit, and suggest you check it out.

The other way we can give our music away is by asking for fans to pre-save a single that we haven't released yet — and in turn for the pre-save, they get early access to that song. For this, I use Distro Kid's Hyper Follow.

You might be really resistant to the idea of giving your music away, and if you are, I invite you to take a second to think about this.

It's not enough to just ask people to pre-save your song. Most people, even if they like what you do, won't pre-save a song because there's nothing in it for them.

But pre-saves are important for us because they help with getting the maximum amount of streams on the day of a song's release.

So, instead of just asking, begging, or pleading for pre-saves, you have to create an irresistible offer which gives your fans the incentive to go ahead and hit the pre-save button.

How? By offering an instant download, plus a couple of bonuses, like the instrumental version, or any other bonus content you want to share. And yes, you read that right. You offer an instant download, even if the song isn't officially released for another couple of weeks, maybe even a month. And keep in mind that the more songs you're giving away and the sexier your offer is, the more likely fans will take you up on it. This means an increase in conversions as well as lower ad costs — which will not just save you money in advertising, but make you more money in royalties over the long term.

I know what you're thinking. *Won't this leak the song early and mess up my launch if I give it away?*

This is where I have to get really real with you. I hate to burst your ego bubble, but right now, barely anyone knows who you are. Your problem isn't leaking the song to a few hundred or even a few thousand fans. Nobody knows you exist right now, a few thousand people getting your song for free is not going to mess up your release. It's going to give you a much better chance of success.

Spotify currently has 165 million users. I have a million monthly listeners on there, which means there are 164 million who have no idea who I am.

The problem for the majority of artists isn't a song being leaked, it's the fact no one knows who they are — and that's what we're working on here, and throughout this whole book. Getting you the attention, the fans and the streams.

Be generous with your fans, and notice how they give back. You're more likely to get shares and to be added to listener-created playlists, which over the course of my career have generated me over one million streams and counting. All by giving away your music in exchange for a save.

Before we move into the next chapter I just want to share a little more on the subject of playlists. This time we're looking into independently-curated playlists, and also artist-created playlists, which you can create yourself.

Independently-curated playlists

If you do a quick search on Spotify for your style of music you'll quickly see there are playlists which cater for every type of genre and mood. These are the playlists which aren't created in-house at Spotify, but by listeners, professional companies, record labels, or even celebrities. Some of these playlists have huge reach and potential to bring new people to your music.

There are thousands of personalized playlists with massive amounts of followers, and you can reach out to these playlists and pitch your songs. It's a big deal when someone adds your song to a playlist. While you might not get a ton of plays right away, those few hundred plays start to add up over time.

Start by researching Spotify playlists based on your genre. For instance you might type in Folk, West Coast Rap, Christian Rock or Dubstep to see what playlists come up. Another strategy you can use is to type in an artist similar to you to see what playlists have featured their music, and contact that playlist owner. Some playlist owners have their contact details on their profiles. Others don't really want to be found so easily so you have to go digging on Twitter, Facebook and even LinkedIn.

Be careful with any playlists that charge money to be featured on them. Always make sure they are legit and not just filled with a bunch of random songs that don't even include your genre. What's the point of getting added to a heavy metal rock playlist if your song is country? I always double check the playlist to see not just the type of songs but the quality of songs. If I can see this playlist owner is just adding everything and anything then I'll quickly pass.

This is a reminder that we're not just trying to get random streams but streams from people who are real fans of our style of music.

You can do this research yourself, or you can ask someone to help. If you have a band, share the load and get them involved. If you're solo, one strategy I teach is to call in help from your mom or another family member, or go ahead and hire a virtual assistant. The task is to look up these playlist owners and build a database of potential contacts for you. If you choose to hire a virtual assistant, try Fiverr or Upwork. As an artist and also the CEO of your company, you need to stop doing 'minimum wage activities', so hire those tasks out to someone else and you can focus on a higher-leveraged activity. I share more about this on my Spotify 5-Day Challenge you can join at https://www.10xyourfanbase.com/livechallenge

When you know who the top playlisters are, reach out to them. Some of these playlists are corporate, so always be professional in how you approach them.

There are also companies who specialize in reaching out to playlisters on your behalf (for a fee), but be careful and make sure they are reputable and have a good track record. Always do your due diligence before just handing over your money. One advantage of this route is that these companies already have relationships with playlisters. There's also the fact that these things can be time-consuming, and as I said a couple of paragraphs ago, you might prefer to spend your time writing more hit songs, shooting videos, or touring.

The first company I hired I met at a conference, which is another reason I always recommend that my students go out and meet people to get their music heard and to build industry relationships.

And don't be afraid of reaching out to celebrities who have playlists; you can do this via social media, or send an email. Don't ever discount cold emailing someone because you never know until you try! My virtual assistant spends an hour a day reaching out to genre-specific social influencers that might want to promote my song or share it to their followers. I'm amazed at the responses I get every day from people responding positively and tagging me on social media when they share one of my songs. You might just be surprised by who'll respond to you when you reach out to them.

In short, either invest the time yourself, or invest your money and hire someone to get onto these playlists for you. I always look at something like this as a long-term investment for building my fanbase.

And the beautiful thing is, once a fanbase is built, it's built. Then when you release future songs you get traction much faster because you've laid those strong foundations.

When an entrepreneur starts a business they always have a 3-5 year time horizon. I encourage artists and musicians to adopt the same mindset with the songs they release. Focus on a song long enough for it to take off. Don't just release a song and then 48 hours later move onto the next one. I think it's imperative artists focus on promoting the song for 3-5 months to give it a chance to gain traction. I know we all want results fast and when we don't see something working we can easily want to move on. But releasing a song isn't like popping a pain pill and getting a result, but more like a seed you plant. Nurture it and watch it grow.

Artist-created playlists

The last thing I want to look at here are the public playlists you can create yourself as an artist, which can be followed by anyone who has a Spotify account. I've created a few of these, and have found they're a great way to get more exposure for my songs.

Here's an example. One of my public playlists is called Manafest & Thousand Foot Krutch, because I'm friends with the band and we've recorded a lot of songs together. What's cool for me is that they have a much larger fanbase, which I tap into with this playlist I created. This personalized playlist has 1107 followers, and has brought me almost 50,000 streams to date.

Now, if you happened to be an artist who's also recorded with Thousand Foot Krutch, you could get in touch with me and ask if I'd consider adding you to this playlist, and if I like the song, I might give it a shot. Then 1107 people may get a chance to hear a new song has been added to that playlist they follow — resulting in more exposure for all of us. But can I just request that you don't email me asking to be added to this playlist! I'm sharing the example here as way to demonstrate my point, and to get you thinking outside the box.

So here's a challenge for you. What if you made a playlist that's a mix of your own music with someone else's, choosing a band or artist who has a similar sound to you? I sometimes get compared to Papa Roach so I could create a playlist made of my songs and their songs. And the point of this? So when people are searching for Papa Roach, they find my playlist too — meaning they find me too. You could do this with TV shows, movie soundtracks or even gaming playlists. This is how you tap into an already established ecosystem of fans. This is what I call making yourself findable on Spotify.

What if we were to look at Spotify as a really powerful search engine? I have to say, I think that's exactly what it is. It's free exposure and a huge opportunity to get more listeners. This truly un-tapped area of Spotify is something I'll expand on in the next chapter.

I hope what you're starting to tune into here are the possibilities of cross-pollinating and connecting with other artists as co-creators rather than seeing them as competition.

The next chapter is all about that: we're going to look at how collaborations and cover songs can accelerate your streams and keep expanding your all-important fanbase.

Chapter 7:

EXPANDING YOUR FANBASE: COLLABORATING TO SUCCESS

I tell all my students that I coach one on one that collaborating with other artists and producers is the fastest way to grow their fanbase, receive royalties, and accelerate their music career.

My biggest song, *Impossible*, with over 38 million streams, was a collaboration. Not only did I work with two other songwriters to pen it, but the song itself has a featured artist, Trevor McNevan of Thousand Foot Krutch, singing the chorus.

The big reason why collaborating with other artists is so powerful is because you get to tap into that artist's existing fanbase. And if they have a bigger fanbase than you — even better. When you work with another artist it's like getting their rubber stamp of approval, and the message that goes straight to their fans is this: *Hey, check out this guy or girl's music.* That's powerful, and the effects can be instant. One artist I know paid for a collaboration and went from 24,000 monthly listeners to 40,000 within 48 hours of that new song coming out. You couldn't spend enough on advertising to get that kind of instant result.

One way to think about this is to imagine the difference between someone recommending a product to you personally, versus you seeing the advertising online or receiving a marketing email about it. You're way more likely to dismiss the advertising or the email than you would your friend's recommendation, because as humans we value and appreciate other people's opinions.

When I first started out as a musician, I cold-emailed a record label for years and got no response. Then an artist who was already signed to the label introduced me to the president. He gave him my demo and played him my songs, and I had a recording contract in my hands within months when previously nothing had happened for years.

That's the power of an introduction.

Yes, you can grind it out alone online, you can saturate social media, you can pay for ads and you can do a ton of touring.

Or ... you can buy your way in by paying for a collaboration.

Of course, it's not as simple as either/or. I'm not saying that you don't need to do the other stuff, the hard work and the grind is all a necessary part of your journey as we've been exploring, but collaborations are a phenomenal way to fast track your way to success. There are very few other career moves you can make where you'll get introduced to a potentially huge fanbase overnight.

In essence, when you collaborate, you're integrating into the other artist's business, and vice-versa. And that integration lasts. It's a long-term investment that you'll both benefit from for years to come. It should be every artist's goal to build a sustainable business, and you can do this not just by relying on your own fanbase, but also by connecting with some of the tens of thousands of others that are available.

And while there is usually a financial cost involved, especially when you're starting out, it's so worth it. You have to be prepared to pay your collaborator, so use part of your marketing budget to invest in this.

See collaborations as high-end, high-impact marketing. The truth is, the goal of any financial investment you make in yourself should be to get you to your desired goal faster — and collaborations do that for you. Not only are you getting a powerful referral to another fanbase, but every time someone checks that artist out there's a great chance they'll find you too. It's the search engine comparison again. The more you show up in Spotify's search results, the more streams and royalties you'll get paid.

Let me tell you a little story. It's one of regret. A few years ago, there was one artist I was going to do a collaboration with, but I didn't push to make it happen. The truth is I sent him a song and he wasn't really feeling it, and instead of me following up and sending him another song I got lazy. I neglected to remember a key piece of advice I teach: the fortunes are in the follow up. Anyway, fast-forward to today and that artist now has over 13 million monthly listeners. I could have tapped into that artist's insane growth if we had done a song together, but I missed out on that opportunity. You live and learn!

Before we get deeper into the specifics of setting up a collaboration, here's something else I find really cool about working with other artists. Not only are you getting introduced to their fans, but you are likely to get access to their whole network of connections in the music industry, including the other artists who follow them. Maybe you've heard the phrase 'Your net-worth equals your network' — and this is so true. The more connections you have, the more opportunities will open up and be made available to you.

I've met Spotify promotion companies, synch companies, graphic designers and more all from collaborations I've done. What's really cool too is that I get to see how that artist's team works, and the different strategies they utilize to market songs. This is gold! So often I'll learn a new way of reaching people or getting creative with marketing that I never would have considered on my own. I love growing and learning, and rubbing shoulders with other movers and shakers keeps me fresh and inspired.

Now we've looked at all the reasons why collaborations are accelerators of success, lets look at how to approach this process.

It's all about strategy, my friends!

Begin with the end in mind

When you're choosing who you'd like to collaborate with, you need to be strategic, so there are a few things you want to be thinking about. There's a really useful saying that applies here and it's this: *Begin with the end in mind.*

Why this artist? What can they bring to your song? What's the end goal here?

Obviously, you want to be working with someone whose music you like and who you believe will compliment your style and suit the song you want them to feature on. They don't have to be making music in the same genre as you, in fact, a cross-genre collaboration can be a really effective curve ball if the song is awesome. Think Eminem and Dido, Linkin Park and Stormzy, Metallica and Lou Reed... There are heaps of examples like this, and both fanbases love it when you throw out something unexpected like that.

Other factors you want to be thinking about are, of course, the number of monthly listeners the artist has on Spotify — that's an obvious one. As a rough guide, if you're an artist with 1,000 monthly listeners or less, I'd advise you to collaborate with two or three artists who have 5,000-10,000 monthly listeners. The cool thing about getting a bigger artist on your song is you can literally run Facebook, Instagram and even Spotify ads directly to their fanbase. That's a ready-made crowd of interested people who will very likely click on those ads to check out a song from a band they already like, while simultaneously discovering you. That's pretty cool! We've got more on how to run ads coming up later in the book.

When choosing who to collaborate with you also want to check out how active their social media is, and in particular see if they're doing well on a platform which you haven't totally got into yet. I've had collaborations where I have a bigger Spotify following than my co-creator, but they're doing better on Instagram or TikTok. This way we scratch each other's backs and hack both of our fanbases — especially when we go live together to promote the song, which is another strategy in itself. More on that in Chapter Nine.

The key here is that there should be a reason you want to get that collaboration. Yes, to grow your fanbase, but also — what will that growing fanbase give you? Think about the doors you want to open by having a certain number of monthly listeners. When you're hitting the bigger numbers it's so much easier to approach festivals and booking agents, to get labels to notice you, and to even catch the attention of other artists. Now that I have a million monthly listeners, I use that to open up doors that I couldn't back when I had 100,000 monthly listeners.

And if those numbers seem intimidating to you right now, don't worry. You're already on your route to growth by reading this book (as long as you're trying out and implementing the methods!) and we still have a ton more to look at, like running Spotify ads to get your numbers up.

So the point right now is this: have your end in mind. Keep it in your sights and use it to motivate you. This is where it helps if you have one year, two year and three year goals in mind that you're working towards. Many artists overestimate what they can get done in a few months, yet underestimate what can be accomplished in three years. Expand your vision out, just like those entrepreneurs who have a 3-5 year time horizon.

Here's an example from my own experience where I had the bigger picture in sight when choosing who to collaborate with.

A while back I really wanted to get more radio play on a bunch of active rock radio stations in the USA, so I chose to work with an artist who was getting plays with those stations. I knew that just being associated with this artist would be good for me. Because he was already getting airplay, the stations were happy to play the song we created together. And then, because I'd got an 'in', it was easier for me to get my own songs added into rotation on these stations.

Everything is leverage when you're first getting started. You want to make it easier for the gatekeepers to say yes, and harder for them to say no.

On the subject of getting the attention of radio stations, what I'm about to share isn't related to collaborations but I'll share it because I think you'll get a kick out of the story, and it's good advice that you can adapt and use yourself if you want to.

In Chapter Four, we looked at getting onto editorial playlists, and I suggested sending gift packages through the mail to any curator at Spotify who you want to impress and connect with. Well, you can do that with radio stations too (and anyone in the industry, in fact).

A while ago, Killian, a cologne brand who I really like, brought out a fragrance called Black Phantom, and I love that scent. It's expensive at $400 a bottle, but it came in this really cool black box with a skull on the top, which is really aligned with the design of my own brand. I just thought it was awesome. So I had the idea to buy a bottle of this super-expensive fragrance and send it to a certain radio station which I knew had a huge reach, and in the box I added a USB key pre-loaded with the song I wanted them to play. I also included a little handwritten note as an extra touch.

I'm proud to say it worked! The song did get added, it was heard all across the USA, Canada and New Mexico, and the royalties were ten times my investment.

If this kind of marketing appeals to you, go for it. Put yourself out there, get noticed, and stand out for all the right reasons.

One final tip about radio play. Just as you're being discerning about who you collaborate with, take care to choose radio stations with a good reach. The goal is to get you in front of (or in the ears of) as many people as possible, so be wise and go for the stations that play your kind of music and can get you the best exposure.

Okay, back to collaborations! Next up let's look at the often tricky area of money and negotiations. If you want me to spend a week with you answering your questions and focusing on your Spotify then get a VIP ticket to our next 5-day challenge: https://www.10xyourfanbase.com/livechallenge

Have a game plan

When you've decided on the artist or artists you'd like to work with, the next step is to reach out and ask them if they'd consider collaborating with you. It's pretty easy these days to find the contact details of a band or solo artist as long as they have an online presence, which is pretty much everyone in the industry. Look them up, get their email address, and hit them up. You can also DM them on Twitter, Facebook, Instagram, TikTok, or you can connect via LinkedIn. I've also found it very helpful going to a song I like on Spotify and clicking the three dots beside the song and pulling up the song credits, which allows you to see the names of the producers and songwriters of that song. So if you can't get hold of the artists, try reaching out to the producer and slowly work your way in. You can even look up their manager's details, or their booking agent's details, and get in touch that way.

When reaching out to anyone in the music industry always be short, clear and get to the point quickly. Here's an example of a DM I've sent before: *Hey, I love the new song you just released! Would you be down for a collab?*

This works too: *Hey, I love your stuff, and have a song you'd sound awesome on! How much do you charge for a feature?*

And please, never send an email with an attachment — send any files via Dropbox or a service like WeTransfer, or even a link to an unlisted audio on Soundcloud or YouTube.

So the point is there are multiple ways of reaching out and you just have to start somewhere. And be persistent! If you don't get an email reply, try socials. I like to give it three or four days after contacting someone before I try again. I urge you to get brave and go after it! If you really want this collaboration, persevere.

The other thing to consider is you want to have a number in mind of how much you'd like to spend, or how much you can spend. When I reach out for collaborations, I sometimes begin by asking the artist what they charge for a feature. That number could be anywhere between $500 and $20,000, plus a percentage of publishing and master, depending how big they are, and how big the feature is.

So there's a lot of variety when it comes to what price to pay for a collaboration. You could get someone with a couple hundred thousand monthly listeners for $500 or less. Anything above 300,000 listeners expect to pay $1000 and up, but it always depends on the artist and how into the track they are. Remember the bigger you are in terms of fame, monthly listeners, and fanbase size, the easier it will be to get artists interested. If they don't mention an amount when you ask, say what your budget is and ask if that's something they can work with.

When you get into the negotiations, my advice is to be careful not to over negotiate. Whenever I've been in the position of being asked by another artist to do a feature, I've had a couple of experiences where they've tried to get the price right down or been a little too pushy for my liking, and it starts to leave a sour taste in my mouth. So don't be that guy. Remember you are coming to them for the feature which is some of the best marketing dollars you'll ever spend, so this is not the right time to be penny pinching.

The point is be cool. If the artist you want to work with is asking for $5000, sure, see if you can get them down to $4000. But if they say no, be respectful and take it. The last thing you want is to over negotiate to get them for a cheaper price, but then find they don't want to appear in the music video, or they're not interested in promoting the song on their social media and so on because you essentially beat them up on price so much.

If you don't have the funds to pay your artist, you might negotiate no fee and just offer publishing royalties and / or a split of the master.

Overall, be prudent in who you choose to work with. If you're paying a fee, only send 50% of it upfront, not the full amount. That way you won't get into a situation where someone takes your money then you're waiting for them to finish recording vocals for months on end. Get whatever you've agreed on in writing, too. Screen shot the email trail or conversation over social media just in case.

I don't normally bother with contracts or getting lawyers involved because it tends to freak out artists and slow down the process. Also I don't want to waste money on lawyer's fees if I can just work with good people and get it all in writing. This is not legal advice, but the best thing you can do is just to work with good people.

What I love about the digital distributor DistroKid is you can split the master royalties inside the software so that everyone gets paid the agreed-upon amount automatically. I'm not a fan of accounting, I'd rather be creating in the studio, so having access to these types of online tools makes it so much easier for collaborations.

Some artists would rather just get paid a fee right away and not take publishing or master rights, but it's all on a case-by-case basis.

I always like to invest for the long term so I'd rather pay a one-off fee for the feature and keep 100% of the master because that means I'll get paid all the royalties for life. So many artists only think short term and don't realize after one or two years, or even sooner, they could make all their money back and then they're making a profit on that song for the rest of their life.

If you don't have the cash to pay a collaborator, then to get started leverage a piece of the master if you have to. Just don't let anything stop you from moving forward. You are a creator and you'll always be able to write more songs.

I'd just like to say at this point, for anyone who might be thinking of emailing me to ask for a collaboration, I'm only interested in collaborating with artists with 1,000,000 monthly listeners or more. I do, however, wish you luck with your song!

A word of caution

Once the collaboration is finished, recorded, mastered, and ready to release, you need to make sure that when you're setting up the song inside of your digital distributor (e.g. DistroKid or TuneCore) that you make your featured artist a *primary artist* on the song — not just a featured artist — otherwise the song won't show up in their Spotify Artist's dashboard. And if it doesn't show up in their dashboard, they can't pitch the song to Spotify curators. And if they don't pitch it to those curators, the Release Radar won't get triggered, and none of their followers will get notified about the song.

Obviously, that's a huge mistake to make because the whole point of the collaboration is to reach that other fanbase and get as many streams as possible. Can you imagine how frustrating it would be to go through the whole process of creating a song, reaching out to an artist, securing a collaboration, paying the fee, recording the song, getting it ready to go and then making a small mistake like that which will have far-reaching consequences?

I don't have to imagine it, because I did it! And even just writing about it now I could kick myself. Gently. At least I did it so you don't have to!

Luckily, the band I collaborated with still promoted the song to their fans and it did amazing overall, so on the whole it was still worth it. Despite the glitch it got over 2 million streams, but there's no denying I missed out on the main benefit of working with that other artist with that one little admin error.

To get the most out of the situation, we decided to re-release the song, this time as an acoustic version, and this time I really made sure I made the other artist a primary artist in DistroKid! The song sounded awesome and I was excited to share this new version with the world, this time with a proper release on both sides.

However... between that first release and this proposed second release, the artist signed with a record label — and they wouldn't let us release the song. This was so frustrating! And it's one of the reasons I dislike the whole label system. Plus it was pretty narrow-minded of the label because I had over double the audience that this artist had, so I'd be bringing them a ton of new fans, which would obviously benefit the label too. It's insane that they couldn't see that. But it's how that side of the industry is. And that level of control and restriction is one of the reasons I left it behind.

So, we had to rework the song for a third time, this time with me singing all of the vocals.

I guess there are two morals of this story. One is to be prepared and plan ahead, that way if any mistakes are made you have time to rectify them. I didn't get a chance to rectify my mistake, partly because it took me a while to work out what I'd done wrong, and also because we were already close to the release date. This is why I suggest you're submitting your songs a month ahead of the release date.

Also, before we get to lesson number two I just want to say that when doing a collaboration make sure you have agreed upon a release date for the song so it doesn't conflict with any other songs the artist is releasing. If the artist is signed to a label make sure you get permission in writing that you have the rights to release the song so nothing gets in the way. I've heard of artists who paid for a feature only to have the label block it — and they didn't get their money back, either.

And lesson two is that even when things go 'wrong', you can work them out. You can push through, you can get creative and think outside the box. This is your dream, so keep fighting for it!

Cover songs

If you can't collaborate, then cover. It's the next best thing, because it's another way of tapping into a new fanbase. There are countless success stories of artists who blew up when they covered hit songs. Think Joan Jett covering *I Love Rock n Roll, or Run-DMC* doing their version of *Walk This Way*. And we can't forget the famous Gotye track, *Someone That I Used To Know*, covered by the Canadian band Walk Off The Earth. Check out their YouTube performance which they called '5 people 1 guitar!' To date, that video has close to 200 million views.

One of my favorite songs is *High Hopes* by Panic at The Disco, who got their start by covering Blink-182 songs. Even some of the biggest bands ever like Nickelback and Nirvana also performed cover songs before getting their big break. Coming from Canada, I remember Justin Bieber got his start sitting out front of public areas, strumming his acoustic guitar and singing covers of songs.

So how does doing a cover of a song that's already a hit for another artist help you grow on Spotify?

It's pretty simple, and it goes back to something we looked at in Chapter Six: Spotify is a search engine. Let me show you what I mean.

One of Adele's earliest hit songs from back in 2008 was *Make You Feel My Love*, which, you may or may not know, was a cover of a song originally by Bob Dylan. Now, if you're a Dylan fan, and you want to hear that song, and you search for it on Spotify, it's not his version that comes up first — it's Adele's. Adele's version currently has over 875 million streams.

Isn't that crazy? When you search in Spotify for that song title, the cover shows up as the number one result instead of Bob Dylan's original version. In fact, his is fourth on the list, with 22 million streams. Obviously that's still a lot of listens, but compared to 875 million, it pales in comparison.

So doing a great cover will not only help you to tap into an artist's fanbase, but it'll get you showing up in one of the biggest search engines you can appear in.

If you want to try this out for yourself, my advice is to make a list of hit songs that you could cover, and then go for it, starting with the one you're most excited about. Of course, do it well. Don't just rush out an acoustic cover without much thought or production value. Put some real effort behind the recording, and see what kind of new twist and personality you can give it. Reimagine something amazing.

Another strategy is to cover a new song that's on its way up the radio or streaming charts and ride its coat tails. There's a story of a rock band, I Prevail, that got a tip from a radio promoter that Taylor Swift was about to release a new single. The band jumped in the studio quick to cover the now-famous Taylor Swift song *Blank Space* just as it was on its way to radio. This helped them get massive exposure because every time fans searched for that song their cover also popped up. Because the cover was done well fans loved it enough to check out the band and they ended up selling tens of thousands more copies of their EP.

It should be noted here that cover songs and collaborations alone can't buy you fans. Even advertising has its limits. All of these things can get you more impressions, but it's your music, and the way you connect with and reach your fans that will convert their hearts.

Finally, the cool thing with covers is that you own 100% of the master, which is the biggest royalty generated compared to the publishing. You didn't write the song so you won't own any of the publishing, but because it's a new recording you will own the master. What's really awesome is DistroKid allows you to upload covers to Spotify, Apple Music, iTunes etc. right from their platform, and as I mentioned previously it handles all the legalities for you, including paying out the publishing fees to the songwriters. There's a small annual fee for this but it's so worth it.

You can find out more on this in my book, *The Truth About the Music Business*.

Chapter 8:

INTRODUCING SPOTIFY ADS

"If you haven't offended someone with your music by noon each day you're not marketing your songs hard enough." — Manafest

We've looked at a multitude of ways you can build your audience with Spotify, some low-cost, some totally free, from customizing your profile, to creating canvases, to releasing your songs via the Waterfall strategy, to getting onto the many different types of playlists, to building a community of fans, to collaborating with other artists, to covering songs that will pull listeners into your orbit.

Now it's time to focus on the world of paid advertising on Spotify.

If you've ever listened to music on Spotify as a non-premium user you'll know what a Spotify ad is. They play around every fifteen minutes between the tracks you're listening to, and they're usually about 30 seconds long.

Now, before we get further into this, let me just say that when you decide to use part of your marketing budget to run Spotify ads, or any kind of ad campaign, you're making a financial investment. And what are you investing in? One of the best things you can ever invest in ... yourself! Never lose sight of that. Even buying and reading a book like this is an investment, not an expense. It's the same with any courses or classes you decide to enroll in, or mentorships you participate in. So yes, there's a cost involved here, but when we're considerate about how we use the money we're investing, we're way more likely to come out on top.

The question isn't, *How much is it gonna cost me to run Spotify ads? But rather, How much is it gonna cost me if I don't?*

Playing the long game

Something to be aware of with running ads, especially Spotify ads, is that you might not get an instant ROI (return on investment) in the first few months — or even the first six months — so you have to recognize that this is about the long game. It's about building momentum so that fans, new and old, continue to stream your music and earn you royalties for life. Believe me, I've marketed my music for years and now I'm happily reaping the benefits. Like I said way back at the start of the book, when someone buys a CD they pay you once and can listen for a lifetime. With Spotify if a fan streams you every day for ten years you get paid on every single one of those streams.

I've been marketing and promoting my music for years, both in this new era of connecting and reaching people online, and via the old organic way with going on the road and touring. As such, I've built a strong and dedicated fanbase. Now I have so much momentum from my previous work that I don't have to promote my songs as much, and I still make multiple six figures from my music.

This is why the artist lifestyle is so coveted: when you write and record hit songs they'll earn you royalties for life. That's why it helps to look at your career in the music industry as a long-term adventure as opposed to something you're just trying out.

In fact, notice the difference between the idea of *trying* to do something versus *deciding* you're going to do it.

When you decide something, there is a sense of finality and commitment. There are no other options. As I like to say: there's no plan B.

Trying, on the other hand, has a sense that sure, you'll give it a shot, but if you face any difficulties, challenges or obstacles, you'll quit.

A try is a fail every time. Stop trying and start committing.

When you commit to investing in your career with paid advertising, you'll really start building your brand awareness — and that's how you'll get your music heard by more people, and it's how you'll create that long, rewarding and prosperous career that I know you want.

Why Spotify ads — and how do they work?

There's no doubt that one of the best things that you can do to keep your Spotify numbers going up is by running Spotify ads. Later, we're going to look at Facebook and Instagram ads too, but right now I want you to tap into the idea that we run Spotify ads because we want to fish where the fish are. When you run ads on another platform like Facebook or Instagram, you're targeting a potential fan who might not even have a Spotify account or be interested in getting one. This is a higher-risk use of your marketing dollars, because even if a fan does have the Spotify app on their phone or computer and they click on your ad to listen to your song, they might not be signed in to Spotify or know their username and login. This is why, if you run Facebook and Instagram ads, you might see your ad getting a lot of clicks but the numbers don't add up to streams, because the people clicking never actually logged in to Spotify to hear your song.

However, when you run an ad on Spotify, you are targeting a fan that is already on the Spotify platform listening to music, and that's a powerful place to start from.

How to begin

The first thing to do to get started with creating ads on Spotify is to create an account. Obviously you already have your Spotify artist account, but you also need to sign up with Spotify ads. To do that, head to adstudio.spotify.com and sign up from there. If they don't have Spotify ads in your country yet, one workaround is to get a VPN and purchase a USA credit card.

There are currently three types of Spotify ads you can create: audio, plus horizontal and vertical video ads.

You'll see that to create your ad, you'll be asked to upload a 640 X 640 pixels image, a click-through url, and for the audio ad only, a voice over. These are the three main components of your ad. If you'd like Spotify to do the voice over for your audio ad, that's an option too and it costs you nothing, plus you get to pick out the voice actor yourself, whether that's female or male, and you can also select the language you'd like. Sometimes I get Spotify to create the voiceover with my music, and then I take that audio and use it for one of my video ads. If any of this sounds confusing just log in to your Spotify ads account and it will all make sense. The best learning comes from taking action. But let's keep going!

Something to keep in mind when you're writing your ad script is this: it's extremely important that you have a call to action in your ad. Why? Because it increases your clickthrough rate (CTR).

For example:

Hey, are you looking for more rock like you just heard? Then check out Manafest and his song Impossible. Click listen now.

To adapt that script for your own ad, here's the template:

*Hey, are you looking for more **[Insert your genre]** like you just heard? Then check out*

***[Insert your artist name]** and their song **[Insert your song name]**. Click listen now.*

If you want more help beyond this book on setting up Spotify Ads then download my Spotify Ad Templates and training at: https://smartmusicbusiness.com/spotifyadtemplates

When it comes to the content of your ad, there are three main things we're going to look at that you can promote with a Spotify ad: your music, tickets to a show you have coming up, or your merchandise. In this chapter our focus is on promoting music, then we'll look at Spotify ads to promote tours and merch in the following two chapters.

In terms of the cost involved, there's a minimum budget of $250 USD per ad, running over a certain number of days for that same fixed price. If you start with $250 and have your ad set up to go for fourteen days, then you're looking at $17 a day. However, if you start the ad and decide it's not working after 24-72 hours has passed, you can stop the ad and you'll only be charged what has been spent so far.

I always suggest to wait at least three days for the ad to run so you can get some data to see how the ad is performing, specifically the CTR. If it's lower than 1% then you might need a different ad creative or you might need to take a look at your targeting.

I suggest you plan to run ads for 30-60 days, spending $250 minimum for 30 days, and $500 minimum for 60 days. A lot of artists want to see a big impact on streams but you have to be willing to invest big money to get the impressions that will make a difference.

Once you've decided to run an ad, it's time to think about the song you're going to promote. As an artist I know you enjoy the buzz of releasing new music and maybe you have something in the pipeline that you want to get traffic on, but my advice is that you start your journey into Spotify ads using the music you already have. Market that first, starting as soon as you can, so that you can get new fans listening. This way, when you release that new material you'll have a fanbase interested, amped and ready to check it out.

As far as the link goes that you want new fans to click on, Spotify recommends you send fans to your profile, album or a playlist. The reason they suggest this is so that once they've finished listening to your song, another one on your profile, album or playlist will play next instead of another artists song. If you set up the ad and just link directly to the song, you're missing a trick and you potentially will not get nearly as many streams.

I tell my students to create a 'This Is [your artist name]' playlist and add their catalogue to it. Whatever song you're promoting add that song to the top of the playlist. Please understand your new 'This is [your artist name]' playlist is different than the one Spotify will eventually create for you automatically once you get thousands of monthly listeners. It's important to create your own playlist because then you control it 100% and can add new songs to it when you release them and get a ton more streams because fans are following it. Look at the creation of this playlist as building a promotional asset.

When I released my latest cover song of *Crawling* by Linkin Park I immediately added it to my own 'This is Manafest' Spotify playlist and it got 2317 streams because I have a ton of fans that follow that playlist. It got more than the algorithmic Spotify playlist that Spotify created for me.

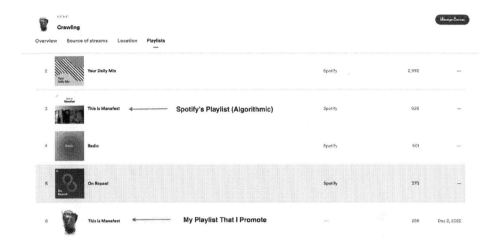

Get into the mindset that running ads isn't a one-time thing, in fact the only time you should stop running Spotify ads is when you want to stop growing your fanbase or you have other growth strategies, like collaborations, in progress. As Henry Ford says, "Stopping advertising to save money is like stopping your watch to save time."

One last thing I want to say here is that when choosing the image for your ad, I suggest using the same artwork as you've used for the single cover of the song you're promoting. That way, there's consistency, and when new fans click over to hear the 30-second snippet of the song they just heard, they recognize similar artwork. The photo has to be 640 X 640 pixels, and as I mentioned earlier in the book you can resize any images you have for free with Canva.com.

From cold, to warm, to hot — to scorching

Next up I want to share an important perspective here with you which is integral to growing your Spotify followers and streams, and central to the way you'll market and make money from your music.

Here it is. You need to look at the listeners you're bringing to your music as one of three things: they're either cold fans, warm fans, or hot fans. That's because there's a journey that every fan goes on from not knowing who you are (cold), to knowing you a little (warm) to knowing you a lot (hot). Let's look at this in more detail.

Your cold audience, or cold traffic, are the people who are just about to be introduced to you. They don't know your name or your music — yet.

Your warm audience are those folks who have been introduced to your music, either through a friend, or through your Spotify ads, or some other way you've marketed yourself. They've already listened to your music, liked a few photos on social media and they maybe even follow you. They're warmed up to you. Think about when you meet someone for the first time — or the first couple of times — they might be a little standoffish because they don't fully know you yet. This is the same concept.

Your hot audience are your hardcore fans — the ones who have already bought stuff from you. They're on your email list, they buy your music, buy your merch, they come to your shows.

Now, you may have noticed from the title of this section there's a stage beyond hot: scorching. These are the fans who don't just follow you — they buy everything you drop, including VIP tickets to your show. They're the first ones in line to support your crowdfunding campaigns. These fans haven't just heard about you — they're your tribe! They're hardcore. They buy and stream everything you release and they share it, too. As I've said, I call my tribe, a.k.a. my scorching hot fans, my Fighters. Your scorching hot fans aren't just fans of your music, but a fan of you.

When you look at it this way, you see that every fan you ever have will take that journey, from not knowing your music, to knowing it a little, to really digging it.

So what does this mean for marketing, and specifically for Spotify ads?

Well, in essence, each of those stages are different, and each group of listeners are different, so you need to treat them accordingly. For example, you wouldn't run an ad promoting an upcoming tour to your cold audience. How likely are they to come and see you if they haven't heard of you? Personally, I enjoy the concerts of artists I know so I can sing along and party with my friends. It's the same thing with merchandise. I'm probably not going to buy an unknown (to me) band's merch unless I happen to really like the design. Same thing with crowdfunding campaigns, it's not very useful to market a crowd funder to new fans. Your existing fans will be way more interested. I tell my students a crowdfunding campaign isn't a fanbase growth exercise, but a fanbase monetizing exercise.

The crux is, we need to be thoughtful about who we're targeting when we run ads of any kind, so start to get strategic in this area.

The bigger picture

Your overall goal with ads should be to create a system that constantly brings in new cold traffic, a.k.a. fans that have never heard of you, because you want to have a pipeline of new listeners coming in regularly so they get a chance to go on that cold to warm to scorching-hot journey with your music. That journey starts when they follow you, and it gets warmer when they eventually purchase your songs.

With that in mind, your aim should be to warm a cold fan up first by running a Spotify ad that will get them to listen to your music first. That's how you start to build the relationship. Think of this like dating someone and getting to know them before you ask them to marry you.

Alongside warming those cold fans up, you also want to be running ads and promoting your songs to fans who already know your music or have heard of you before.

But let's not run before we can walk. For your first Spotify ad I suggest you focus on cold fans to begin with so that you can grow your streams and followers.

Here's how you do it.

Creating your first Spotify ad

Spotify's ad platform allows you to target the fans of any artist on Spotify, so start by making a list of at least ten artists who you sound similar to. You also want those ten artists to have at least 100,000 monthly listeners. If I were doing this, I might start by going to Spotify and selecting Linkin Park, because they're a band I often get compared to.

And this is pretty cool: when I pull Linkin Park's profile up on Spotify and scroll down, I see something called 'Fans also like', and when I check that out, I see a list of other bands and artists.

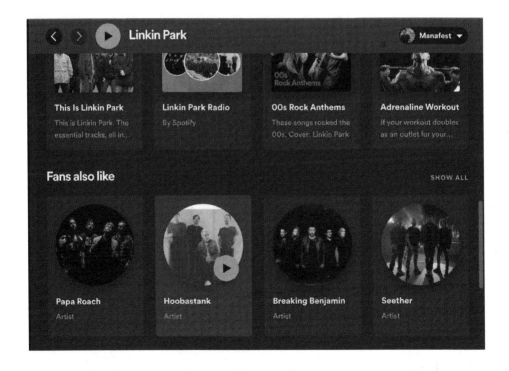

That is super-helpful information, so I highly recommend you use that when you're doing your research; it'll give you more ideas of who to target with your ad.

The whole point of this exercise is that you choose the bands who sound like you, giving you the best shot of warming up someone who likes music that is similar to yours. Don't be tempted to target fans of Taylor Swift or Bruno Mars if you sound nothing like them, just because they have huge fanbases, or even if you're a fan yourself. It's not enough — you have to sound like them for this to be worth your time and money.

Here's a point related to that. As soon as you get over yourself and recognize your music is not for everybody you'll start to win. You don't want to force your music on people who have not raised their hands to say they're interested. Someone once told me, "The riches are in the niches." It's so true. I remember hearing about an interview with a lifeguard who rescues people stranded in the ocean. He was asked, "How do you know who to rescue first?" And he replied, "We go to the people swimming towards us first."

It's the same thing with your fans: focus on the people who are most likely going to want to listen to your music and stop chasing the people that aren't.

Finally, when you know who you're targeting and it's time to upload the content for your ad, think about what you want to say for your voiceover. Going back to my Linkin Park example, If I were targeting their fans I might say something like:

Hey, this Manafest. If you're a fan of Linkin Park or Papa Roach, check out my new song [song name].

Then, naturally, I'd have that song playing somewhere in the ad, too. And not just any part of the song — but the 'best' part. The catchiest part. And when that best part kicks in, it needs to come in clear with no talking over the top.

I ran a split test with two ads for two different songs, investing $250 in each. One of those ads got me 200 new followers while the other grabbed 800+. What did I do differently? I used the chorus in the more successful ad and had a better call to action. Exact same budget for each ad yet I got 4X better response when I used the most attention-grabbing section of the song I was promoting.

Also, when it comes to the voiceover script, keep it short, clear and to the point. You only have 30 seconds and you don't want it to be spent talking. One of my Inner Circle students was talking way too much in his ad, telling this long story about the song. This was the wrong place to do that. I had him shorten it and he got a 10X better CTR and overall performance on the ad.

The music business is a business and you need to treat it as such. Once you get into using ads, test them. Try different songs to see which one pops off. Personally, this is one of the reasons why I love online advertising: it allows me to spend a few hundred dollars and see what's working and what's not. Compare that to radio or publicity campaigns around a song, where you have to commit thousands of dollars just to get started. A lot of newer indie artists don't realize how good we have it. When you have the data of two or three different ads to compare, you can then take the rest of your marketing budget and invest it into the ad that's performing the best.

Don't guess and hope it will work. Instead test, pivot, edit and adjust, and then scale the marketing and promotion of your songs.

And here's something cool you can play with that's totally free: Spotify's popularity score. This score, or index, goes from 0-100 and it indicates how popular your songs are compared to others on the platform. A song with a score of 0 is considered unpopular, while a song with a score of 100 will be one of the most popular tracks on Spotify. So what's the magic number for getting onto playlists? It's said to be 30. To trigger Spotify's algorithm so they start sharing your song in their algorithmic playlists like Radio or Discover Weekly, you need to have a popularity score of at least 30.

There's a free tool called musicstax.com that you can use to look up the popularity score of any of your songs. This is a great tool to use before and after an ad campaign. Use it to check the stats of your song once you've promoted it for a month so you can see how the growth is going and get a clear picture on the impact of your marketing.

Make it your mission to increase your score to help trigger Spotify's algorithm and land on some of those coveted editorial or algorithmic playlists!

Spotify Marquee

Before we wrap this section up I just want to mention another type of ad you can run on Spotify called Spotify Marquee. A Marquee is a full-screen ad that shows up on the Spotify app when users open it and are therefore most likely deciding what to listen to. It's a perfect way to announce you have a new song or album coming out, and because Marquee ads only get put in front of people who have already shown an interest in your music, you have a great chance of getting a clickthrough.

The goal of a Marquee ad is to develop your fanbase further by making lapsed, casual or engaged listeners become even bigger fans of your music than they already are. I always use Spotify Marquee ads as a part of my single or album launch strategy to increase streams and help increase my chances of getting on a Spotify Editorial playlist. Remember the first 24-48 hours of releasing a new song are crucial to its long-term success, so the more streams you can get, the better.

Spotify suggests that this method of advertising is much more effective at driving streams than social media, and that a fan who sees a Marquee is two times more likely to save a track or add it to their playlist, which is very cool indeed!

At the time of writing, Marquee isn't available to all artists: you need to have over 5K streams in the last 28 days, and more than 1K followers, and set your billing to US billing. That last condition can be worked around inside your account, as long as you have a US-based payment card to pay for this service. I'm sure they'll roll it out to all territories eventually, so even if you can't access it now, keep it in mind for the future.

Also, if you don't have the minimum stream requirements or followers on Spotify, then just keep growing your fanbase via all the strategies I'm sharing in this book until you do. The more success you get the easier you will find it is to grow — especially when you have momentum on your side. You'll also get access to a lot of really cool tools. It's at the bottom where it's crowded, not the top — so let that be your incentive to keep climbing!

Chapter 9:

SPOTIFY ADS FOR TOURS AND SHOWS

"Productivity is never an accident. It is always the result of a commitment to excellence, intelligent planning, and focused effort."
— Paul J. Meyer

In this chapter I'm going to demonstrate how you can use Spotify ads on both your cold and your warm/hot audience. A great way to explore this is by looking at how we can use ads to promote any upcoming shows or tours we might have.

The cool thing about Spotify ads, and why they work to promote your shows, is that they can not only put you in front of fans of artists who are similar to your genre of music, but they can also target listeners based on where they live.

That means if you've got a show coming up in Toronto, you can target people who live in Toronto. If you have a show in San Diego, you can target people in San Diego. And then, within the ad itself, there's a link that goes directly to a ticket sales page or tour page.

Whether the show you're promoting is a regular concert, a CD release party, a spot on a festival billing, or even a showcase for a label or booking agent — when you do it right, Spotify ads can help you sell more tickets and get more people down to the venue.

So let's look at how we can do Spotify ads for tours right!

Devising your ads

In the run up to your show or your tour, I advise you to create two ads. I want you to think of these ads as fishing nets, but instead of trying to catch fish we're catching fans.

With Ad #1 you should be casting a bigger, wider net and spending more of your budget. This is because Ad #2 is going to re-target the audience we build off Ad #1, so it's going to a smaller but also more warmed up audience.

Ad #1 is targeted at cold fans who live in the same city or close to the city where you're playing. Remember in the last chapter we said it's not a great idea to try to promote a concert to a cold fan? That still applies here — we're not going to mention the show yet, because our goal with Ad #1 is to get this new fan, who lives close to where you're playing, to listen to your music. That's all. Then a few weeks before the show, when they've become warm fans, we'll target them again, this time with the information about the show.

Ad #2 is for your warm or hot fans who also live in the city where you're playing, and the purpose of this ad is to inform them about your show. They already like you, they're already interested in your music, and this ad is going to entice them to come and see you. When you select the fanbase you're targeting within Spotify Ad Studio, you'll select your own artist name under the fanbase targeting option, and your ad will play between tracks when your fans are already listening to your music.

In terms of timing, you should be running both of your ads at least three months in advance of your show, and then again 3-4 weeks in advance, because the truth is people are often busy, easily distracted, and even when they are interested in you they just might put off checking your link out. Running your ads twice will catch more people and get your ticket page more hits.

Here's a note on how you choose the geographical areas you're targeting for both of these ads. Depending on how big the city where you're playing is, you might want to include the surrounding cities as well because some people are willing to travel — especially if they're your hot audience. I've had fans drive up to six hours to come see me play, especially if that's the only show I'm playing in that state.

So take the time to do your research with this, look on Google maps and notice the cities and towns in the surrounding areas to your venues and include them when you choose the areas your ad will play in, and you'll increase the amount of people you reach.

What to say

The script for Ad #1 can be the same or very similar to the one I gave you in the previous chapter for targeting new fans, and remember we're not mentioning the show in this ad. The only thing that's different here is the cities where this ad will play, and the only call to action is to click on a link that takes them to somewhere they can hear more from you or stream or buy your song.

So we can move to looking at the script for Ad #2. Here's how I'd create the content for Ad #2 if I were playing a show in Toronto.

First off, because this ad is for fans who are already familiar with my music, I'd have one of my biggest hits playing in the ad to grab their attention. Again, you should use the catchiest part of the song, most likely the chorus, the verse or the bridge.

My voiceover would say something like this, and I'd probably split test my voice versus Spotify's voiceover team to see which one performs best.

Hey, what's up? This is Manafest and I'm playing a show in Toronto at Lee's Palace at 9 PM on Saturday, May 25th. You can get your VIP tickets now which includes a signed poster plus meet and greet with the band, just click to learn more and come party with us.

Here's another option which includes information about a special offer. Remember you always want to 'incentivize' fans to buy, so make sure the offer is appealing.

Hey, what's up? This is Manafest and I'm playing a show in Toronto at Lee's Palace at 9 PM on Saturday, May 25th. The first 100 ticket buyers get a FREE CD signed by the band at the door, just click to learn more and get yours before we sell out.

These are just examples, so of course use your own language that fits your voice and your brand. Be friendly, be upbeat, and make an irresistible offer that's so good they can't say no. I have to say I think it's pretty cool that we get to reach out and speak to our fans like this!

Where to take them

Staying with the examples above, the link within my ad could go to a page that looks like the image below.

I build my landing pages with software called ClickFunnels, and if you head to smartmusicbusiness.com/spotifybonuses you can have that template for free.

Notice how in the first ad script I mentioned that VIP tickets were available. VIP tickets are awesome and I totally recommend you offer these to your fans if you can. Not only do they give you the chance to make more money per ticket sale, but fans love them (and so do I) because they build more of a bond and a connection between us. Not all your fans will take the VIP, but a percentage of them will, because it's a much better offer than just a ticket. More on that in a second.

When I offer VIP tickets, I might include early entry to the show, a meet and greet, a photo opportunity, a laminate lanyard, a vinyl and crowd-free merch shopping — which means they get to browse the merch early before everyone else with a regular ticket gets into the venue. All of this really adds to the VIP experience. Plus what do you think your fans will do if they get a photo with you? They'll immediately post it on social media, sharing it with all their friends, promoting you even more.

When it comes to pricing, it's important to make the VIP offer so irresistible that fans find it hard to say no. If I sell a VIP ticket for $25, I'd price the regular ticket at $15, because the extra $10 is really hard to resist when you see all of the bonuses that come with it. People love feeling like they got a great deal, and the VIP ticket is also a way for a hardcore fan to show their appreciation for you and to have an awesome time at your show. I also suggest making the VIP tickets limited, and when you keep selling out you increase the price accordingly.

The order bump

Something else I recommend you think about doing on your ticket page and anything you ever sell online is an order bump. An order bump is when an additional product is added on the checkout page, and with a concert a really cool thing to offer is the chance to buy an extra ticket for a friend. Because who likes to go to a concert alone? Probably nobody, right? And so at the checkout you present your customer with the chance to get a second ticket for a friend for an additional $20. So that's one ticket for $25, and bring a friend for an extra $20.

An order bump will increase your ticket sales just by being there on the checkout page. How cool is that?!

I also do this with our Free + Shipping offers which dramatically increases our AOV (average order value). It's beyond the scope of this book, but this is also what I highly recommend doing when launching a crowdfunding campaign. Businesses leave a ton of money on the table simply by not having an order bump. The best time to invite someone to buy something extra is when they already have their credit card out. For more info on running a successful Crowdfunding campaign, check out my course Crowdfunding Secrets at: https://smartmusicbusiness.com/crowdfunding

So that's how I use Spotify ads to elevate and expand my reach when I'm playing a show or going on tour. I hope you can see the ways you can adapt and use those strategies for yourself, in a way that suits your music and your vibe.

Using Spotify to plan a tour

Before we move onto our final chapter on Spotify ads, and while we're on the subject of tours, I just want to guide your attention to a feature on Spotify which you can use to help you plan the logistics of a tour.

Spotify is famous for all the data it collects from its users, and lucky for us we get to see this data from our artist dashboard and use it to make better decisions in our marketing efforts.

So here's how it works for touring. By the way, this feature is best used when you've released a few songs or albums and your fanbase is building in the thousands.

Head to your Spotify dashboard and check out where your streams are coming from. This priceless data can be the bedrock for planning a tour, as well as helping you be strategic when hitting up radio (by targeting the local stations where you're popular) plus any other promotional activities you have going on.

When you click on the audience tab, you'll see the countries where you're popular, and you'll also see the cities — and that's the information you need. When I look at my data in this way, I see that six out of seven of the cities where I'm most listened to are in the United States, so knowing this, I can pull up a map and start looking at a possible route for a six-city tour.

Then, when I have the route and dates sketched out, I can start looking up venues in those cities and reaching out to book them. In my email I'll explain I've got thousands or hundreds of people listening to my music in their city, and that my fans would love to see me play there, plus I assure them I'll run Spotify and Facebook ads to make sure fans show up. I'd also attach a screenshot of my Spotify data to back up my claims.

Honestly, this is such valuable information to have. I wish I'd had this kind of data at my fingertips when I was planning tours back in the day because I played so many new markets where no one had ever heard of me. It makes so much more sense to build the demand up online first, as opposed to grinding it out on the road.

Whenever and wherever you tour, I suggest only playing cities where you know you have fans (via the Spotify data) unless you're opening up for someone else and pulling from their fanbase.

Also don't bite off more than you can chew: doing a six or seven city tour takes a lot of planning, promotion and risk. What if you just played one sell-out show in your biggest city where you have the most streams? I'd rather have one killer show that was promoted well with a great turn out, than a stressful half-baked tour that was thrown together.

One last tip. The 'listeners also like' feature is super-helpful for touring, too. You can use it to find out who else your fans love and then reach out to some of those artists to ask if they have a following in any of your top cities. And if they do, you can see if they want to do the show together.

Your email could say:

Hey [insert artist name], I saw in my Spotify dashboard that my fans also listen to your music. Would you be interested in doing a show or a mini tour together?

Remember, when we see other artists as collaborators and co-creators we can expand our fanbase overnight.

In fact, you might want to think about doing a collaboration on a song together with any artists you join forces with for a show, not only to feed off each other's fanbase as we've already looked at, but also to add something rad for the live show, too.

Now that really is all for this chapter! If these ideas have got you stoked and you want more about booking successful tours, then come as a VIP to ask questions on my next Spotify 5-day Challenge **https://www.10xyourfanbase.com/livechallenge**

Chapter 10:
SPOTIFY ADS FOR MERCHANDISE

"If you are not taking care of your customer, your competitor will." — Bob Hooey

In this last section on Spotify ads, I'm going to show you how to create an ad to sell merchandise to your fans. As you might expect, your target for a merch ad is going to be your warm or hot fans — those folks who already know you, like you, and are therefore more likely to be willing to spend money on your merchandise.

This means that, just as you did with Ad #2 for tours and shows in the previous chapter, when you select the fanbase you're targeting within Spotify Ad Studio, you'll select your own fanbase. That tells Spotify to only play your ad to people who have already listened to your music.

When you're selecting the country to target, it's worth noting that at the time of writing this book, Spotify only lets you target one country at a time. So, when I'm running a merch ad I always select the USA because that's where the majority of my fans are.

If you don't have at least 10,000 monthly listeners in one country then I would suggest you keep running the cold ads to keep building your fanbase, and progress into ads for merch later.

What to say: Creating an ad for merch

Do you know what the most powerful word is that you can use when marketing anything at all?

It's the word FREE.

Don't be alarmed — I'm still going to help you make money selling merchandise, I really am. We're not going to give away all your merch for free, so just stick with me here!

One strategy I recommend, and use myself, is called a 'Free + shipping offer.'

This is where you give your fans something physical for free, and they just cover the shipping and handling. I do this with my CDs, and mostly in the USA and Canada because I can ship CDs for super cheap using media mail. If you're wondering whether or not people still buy CDs, I sell thousands and thousands every year — so the answer is YES!

Here's how it works out financially. Depending on the quantity I press, CDs cost me about a dollar each to produce. Shipping is two to three bucks, and I charge $7.97. So that's a profit of around three to four dollars per CD, but the secret of making my money isn't in selling the one CD — it's in the up-sells, in other words the order bumps, I have on the additional pages. After someone gives me their credit card details and orders the CD, I present them with a couple of one-click up-sells, like this:

Order Customization...Step 1 of 2

One Time Offer!

Add **3 Stickers**
And Download **"This Is Not The End"** Album
Featuring 10 Songs + 10 Instrumentals

STICKER 3 PACK

To see more of these strategies, visit
https://smartmusicbusiness.com/freefunnel

Another promotion I run pretty regularly is to offer not just a free CD, but also a free fold-out poster too. This costs an extra 10 cents per unit normally.

Here's the script of what I'd say in the Spotify ad to promote that offer:

*Hey, it's Manafest, thanks for listening to my music. I'm doing something really crazy right now — **for a limited time** I'm **giving away** my CD, plus a free fold-out poster. We've only got **limited quantities** so we ask just two orders per household. Click learn more to get your copy **while I still have some left.***

Notice the words and phrases I've put in bold: not only do I emphasize that both the CD and the poster are free, but I also state it's a limited offer and we have limited quantities. People respond well to deadlines, plus there's a little fear of missing out there too, inciting them to take action. Don't underestimate the power of scarcity and fear of missing out. They are extremely powerful in encouraging fans to buy, as long as they're done in a tasteful way.

The link in the ad I just shared with you will take fans to my website using **Clickfunnels.com**, that' where I sell the CD and offer all my up sells. On the thank you page there is also one more offer I make. Remember they've already got their credit card out so this is a great opportunity to offer them even more. On the order confirmation page I say something like:

Thank you so much for your order, because you supported my music, use code Friends20 and get 20% OFF our store Manafestshop.com

I sell a lot of merchandise on my website using Shopify. So just to be clear there are two pieces of software I use, the first one is **Click Funnels** which has the capability of offering the one click up sells after someone makes a purchase, and then on the thank you page I link to my Shopify store which has merchandise.

Like I mentioned way back in Chapter Two, for selling my merchandise I use a print on demand company called Printful which is connected to my Shopify store. They handle all printing and shipping so I don't even have to carry stock or worry about going to the post office. You can sign up for a free account here.

Sometimes I just run an ad to promote my shop, again with the offer of free shipping on all orders over $50. That ad would sound like this:

Hey Manafest fans — for a limited time any order in the ManafestShop will get free shipping. Click learn more now and see some of our brand new designs.

The secret to offering free shipping is that you increase your prices to cover it. In a world with Amazon everyone expects free shipping when they buy, so you want to stay competitive while increasing your average order value. The goal here is to try to get each customer to spend as much as possible, and you do this by offering free shipping on orders above and beyond a certain price, and by offering up sells.

Obviously the truth is shipping is never free, someone is always paying for it, so another way to word your ad would be:

Hey fans, for a limited time get any of our merchandise at a huge discount, plus we pay the shipping for you.

That way there's still value attached to the shipping, but you've already got it covered by working it into the price.

As I've mentioned previously, whenever I release a new song I create artwork around it, and I will usually try to incorporate the single cover artwork into a T-shirt design. When I run an ad on Spotify promoting the new shirt to my fans, I'll say something like:

Hey it's Manafest, if you're digging my new single [name of song] you're gonna love the merch we just created to go with it, check it out in our ManafestShop.

One final tip on merch. If you want to track your sales and learn where your buyers are coming from, use a specific code in the ad. You could say something like this:

Hey it's Manafest. We just got some sick merch done. It's in our ManafestShop. Click Learn More and use code SPOTIFY to get 20% off your order.

That's why when you hear a promotion on the radio, within the ad they usually use specific codes for you to use, so they can track if their ads are getting a good ROI.

So there we have it. We've covered a lot of ground in these last three chapters, and I hope it's got you inspired and thinking about the ways you can use Spotify ads to target your cold, warm, and hot fans.

Next up we're staying in the area of paid ads, this time looking at how we can use Facebook ads to promote you as an artist on Spotify.

Chapter 11:

FACEBOOK ADS FOR SPOTIFY

You may remember back in Chapter Eight I shared that when it comes to ads and growing a fanbase on a specific platform, one of my philosophies is to fish where the fish are. That means if I'm trying to grow on YouTube, I'll run YouTube ads. If I want to grow on Spotify, I'll run Spotify ads. It comes back to this point: there's always friction in any advertising campaign when you try to get people to jump platforms.

However, there's no doubt that millions of people are using Facebook and Instagram every day, so I would be remiss to not tell you to market there to get your music heard — especially when I've used both those platforms to sell 30,000+ albums to strangers.

You just need to know how to run these ads correctly so you're not burning money, and you also need to truly understand what these ads can and cannot do for you.

For example, something else we looked at in Chapter Eight that I want to echo again here is that it's important to know that if you run a Facebook ad which features a link to a certain song on your Spotify page, you might look at the stats for that ad and see you got 1000 clicks — but you didn't get 1000 streams. As we said, that's most likely because those folks who clicked either don't have Spotify accounts or they aren't logged in, and rather than finding their user name and password they moved on. And while it's possible they moved on to Google you, or to check you out on YouTube or Apple Music — that's not something we can measure or know for sure. So there is a certain amount of risk involved when we ask people to jump platforms, in this case from Facebook/Instagram to Spotify, but there are a lot of rewards too, which we'll get to.

And if you haven't already figured it out, for this book, the purpose of running Facebook ads that link to Spotify is to trigger Spotify's algorithm for a song so that it starts sharing your song automatically.

Before we continue with the nuts and bolts of how to do this, there's something to be said here about expectations. What I mean is, what are you willing to put into an ad campaign, and what do you expect to get out of it?

Most artists want to see a massive lift from their marketing efforts, me included. The problem arises if we want to put minimum effort in for maximum results. If we shy away from spending money on promoting ourselves, yet have no problem spending money on recording, mixing and mastering costs, we're missing something. So many artists come to market their music and freak out! They'll think $10 a day on ads is risky, and thousands over an entire campaign is crazy.

If that sounds familiar, it's really important that you recognize you have that mindset and begin to challenge and move away from it. Imagine if you were signed to a label and they said they were only prepared to put a small budget towards marketing and pushing your record — you wouldn't be happy! You'd want them to do everything possible to get your music heard.

Now YOU have to be the label and do that for YOU.

If you'd like one of our artist coaches to personally walk you through help and setup ads for Spotify or Facebook for your music visit: https://www.smartmusicbusiness.com/coaching

Let's look at how, this time in relation to using Facebook and Instagram.

As an FYI: As you probably know, Facebook owns Instagram. Any ad you create with Facebook can also be used for Instagram, so when I talk about Facebook ads you can assume that I'm also talking about Instagram.

A general piece of advice about when it comes to choosing whether to run your ads on Spotify, YouTube, Facebook and Instagram, or anywhere else, is that it's better to master one platform to begin with, especially if you just want to trigger Spotify's algorithm. If you're running multiple ads on different platforms it's hard to track and easily gets overwhelming. Focus on one platform first, see your streams go up, see your popularity score go up (remember that from Chapter Eight?) then expand out into running ads on another platform. In this way, you're building layers of promotion, which you keep stacking on top of each other.

And when you've mastered multiple platforms, and it comes to launching a song, you can go all out, guns blazing, and promote everywhere you can!

Invest big dollars to see big rewards — but start small

It's way too easy to jump into using Facebook ads and blindly start spending your money if you don't know what you're doing. That's why I suggest you start with a budget of $5-10 a day.

I also highly recommend you scale down the amount of songs you record before you scale down your marketing budget. For example, if you have $10,000 to make ten songs and you've also allocated $5000 for marketing, I'd flip that around. I'd suggest you do five songs for $5000 and put $10,000 into the marketing.

Again, we're coming back to the concept of investment: you need to invest so you get the interest and ears of as many people as possible. That's how you make money off your music. How can you make money if no one knows you exist? Facebook ads, when they're done right, let people know you exist.

So let's take a look at what you need to do to get your ad campaign in motion.

Five steps to create a Facebook ad

Step #1

Decide on the song you're going to promote. For this first campaign, you're just going to focus on that one song — but in Step 2 you're going to make three separate video ads for it. The reason you're creating three different videos for one song is so you can see which one performs the best.

Step #2

Create those three different 1-2 minute videos using that song. You might already have made a music video, so use it for one of the ads if you have one. Other ideas are to create a lyric video, or cut together some live concert footage, or just have a slideshow of cool images playing along with the track.

One cost-effective idea (while still looking really good) is to perform your song at sunset or sunrise and capture that magical background. Do some scouting around your city and find the locations that would suit your song. Bring a few outfits to record a bunch of content, not just for the ads, but also to test out on social media.

Most singles tend to be longer than a couple of minutes, so you'll need to select a section of the song for your ads — so choose an exciting part of it.

Step #3

If you haven't already, create that personal playlist on Spotify called 'This is [Your artist name]' that I advised you do in Chapter Eight. Remember that this is different than the one that Spotify may create for you because you own and control it. Once the playlist is created, add your best songs or whole catalog to it, making sure the song you're promoting is close to the top. Make it either the first or second track on the playlist.

Step #4

Make a list of four or five bands or artists that you sound similar too. I've asked you to think about this a lot throughout the book so I know you're ready for this! Be honest with yourself and don't stretch too far, but come as close as you can and stay within your genre.

My five artists are Linkin Park, Papa Roach, Three Days Grace, Limp Bizkit and Breaking Benjamin. Now, I don't sound identical to those guys, but there's a good chance that fans who listen to those artists might love my songs too.

Using Spotify to look up an artist you sound like and then scrolling down to see 'other artists fans like' is a great research tool that we mentioned previously. This time we're making the list because these are the bands we're going to target inside of Facebook ads manager.

If you haven't done this yet, now is a good time to go to **Facebook. com/adsmanager** and create an account and add a credit card so you can start running paid advertising.

Step #5

Once you're inside Facebook ads manager and ready to create your first ad, you'll be asked what your campaign objective is, and I recommend you choose 'link clicks'. That means Facebook will optimize your ad by showing it to people who are most likely to click on it.

The next thing Facebook is going to ask you is who you want to target in terms of age range, between 14 and 65+. This is where you need to understand your demographics. Typically, I target in the 18-55 range for cold traffic going to my music on Spotify, but whenever I'm trying to run ads to sell something like band merchandise or CDs, then I target 25+ because they are more likely to have a credit card.

Something else you'll decide here is how big your audience should be. My advice is to shoot for a two million audience size minimum, and scale from there as your ad optimizes. By optimizing, Facebook needs 50 conversions a week minimum from an objective to fine tune so they know who to put your ad in front of. Facebook Conversion ads let you know when a fan has taken a specific action like pre-saving your song, giving you their name and email, or making a purchase.

Facebook is constantly collecting dozens of data points about your fans as soon as your ad starts running, and it will optimize to show it only to a portion of those two million people. This is what the Facebook Pixel is for; it's a piece of code you put on your website or landing pages, wherever you are asking fans to pre-save your song or collect their name and email.

It's too advanced for this book, but your ad will eventually burn out and you'll have to have another ad creative on deck to try. Ads start to burn out when you hit a frequency of 1.5-2 which means everyone you've targeted has now seen the ad 1-2 times — which means time for a new ad creative. Generally, you'll know this is starting to happen because ad costs are going up, and in this example, your cost per click starts to rise.

In this chapter I'm giving you the overall strategy on how to run Facebook ads to Spotify, but for video walkthroughs and one-on-one training, including Q&A sessions, I encourage to join our Spotify 5-Day Challenge at **10xyourfanbase.com/livechallenge**

Something else you'll be thinking about at this point in the process is the cost per click, and naturally your instinct might be to go for the cheapest, but it's not always about that. Sure, you can get clicks currently as low as 1-2 cents each, which is fine if you're just targeting third world countries like the Philippines, Brazil or Turkey. That's a good way of split testing your ads for a lower price, and getting some social proof (shares, likes and so on) on your ads, but I recommend targeting in your own country where you have the best chance of playing a local show and recouping your money. It's important to build a fanbase in a country where someone will actually pull out their wallet and purchase something from you one day. And as an FYI, the five biggest markets are USA, Canada, Germany, UK and Australia.

So while you'll be paying more per click, if you're running a great ad it's worth it for the streams, followers and new fans you're connecting with.

Get their attention, and get the click

When you're creating your ad, you want to aim to do two things: grab the viewers' attention, and have a call to action that will make them click your link.

Here are some examples of the text I've used in Facebook ads myself. Although these ads didn't link to Spotify, you can still use them to get inspiration and insights. I give a mini-breakdown of each one so you can see what the important takeaways are.

Most underrated rock artist 'Manafest' is giving away 10 of his new songs for FREE. Download now!

https://hypeddit.com/manafest/saveyouspotifychallenge

Ad breakdown: I said, 'Underrated' to spice it up and get attention. Notice I called out my genre as well, and of course made it clear what's in it for the fans. They're getting 10 songs and most of all they're FREE!

For fans of Linkin Park! Check out rock artist 'Manafest' and download his hit song 'Firestarter' for FREE!

https://www.manafest.com/freefirestarter

Ad breakdown: In this one I used another famous artist to give new fans an idea of what I sound like. You could say, *For fans of The Beatles / Adele / Drake, etc.* And of course I used the magic word FREE.

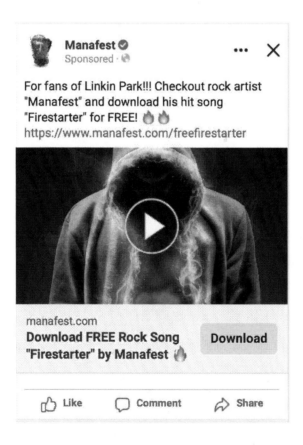

Here's one more example, in which I call out my genre and use the magic word FREE once again:

Hey rock fans! Check out rock artist 'Manafest' and download his hit song 'Firestarter' for FREE!

https://www.manafest.com/freefirestarter

The links in your ad should go to that Spotify playlist we mentioned in Step #3. Once again, the reason we link to a playlist rather than an individual song is to increase the chance that the listener will stay and listen to more than one track. Remember to have the song you're promoting at the top of the playlist, so they know they've reached the right artist page.

In essence, the better your Facebook ad the more likely fans are to share and comment. When this starts happening things can really blow up, and this is one of the reasons why I like Facebook ads — because some of the videos I've run there have got 2.5 million views, 40,000 comments and 2.5K shares.

A good sign that your ad is performing well is when you start to get likes, comments and shares. Just remember even if your ad does really well with kind comments, you're guaranteed to get some hate too, so just accept it and don't let it stop you.

Here's one of my favorite hater comments. You just have to learn to laugh! But it's pretty cool when you get your fans defending you as well, as happened here.

So what makes a great Facebook ad?

It goes without saying that the song you're promoting needs to be awesome. That's just a given. Likewise, the videos you create need to be super cool and in keeping with whatever your style is as an artist.

You also want to think about the thumbnail you choose: it's the picture that scrollers see first so it has to be eye-catching. In fact, it has to grab people by the throat and pull them into your ad!

Pay attention to the copy (the written aspect) of the ad too, and be willing to say something a little out of the ordinary. Me claiming I'm the 'most underrated rock artist' a few pages ago is an example of that! I knew that would rub some people the wrong way, and that I'd get attention by being so bold. It was my aim to get a reaction like, *Who does this guy think he is saying that?* Which would likely lead to a click-through out of curiosity, and also maybe the fear of missing out.

So be bold with your ad!

And here's a bonus tip for if, or when, you run an ad to encourage people to pre-save your song, which is something we covered in Chapter Six. Like I said back then, it's not enough to just ask people to pre-save your song. I hate to say it but no one wakes up thinking, *I can't wait to pre-save a song from an unknown artist!*

So we have to incentivize people in our ad, and we do this by creating a can't-say-no offer.

What if, instead of saying pre-save my song, you changed it to:

Pre-save my song and get it now.

Okay, that's not bad.

How about:

Pre-save my song and get it now plus 9 other songs.

That's better!

But this one:

Pre-save my song and get it now plus 9 other songs and get entered into a contest to win a merch bundle and a $25 Amazon gift card.

Now we're talking!

You've always got to think from a fan's perspective, which is along the lines of, *What's in this for me?*

Use this type of copy in your ad and you'll see your ad costs drop because you're getting way more people to opt in.

Why we run at least two ads at once

I recommend you always run two to three Facebook ads at a time — that's why I suggest you make two to three videos for one song and two to three different thumbnails. Your daily spend of $10 stays the same, but Facebook will automatically split test them and after a few days give the majority of your budget to the one that's performing best.

For example, say you have two ads and you're spending $10 a day. For the first two days Facebook will allocate the money evenly to see which ad gets the most clicks. Then, when it learns whichever ad is performing the best, it will automatically start spending the majority of your budget on that ad.

That way you, as a marketer, are getting a good return on investment from your marketing dollars, and also the user is getting served the best ad. Facebook cares about you as the marketer, but more importantly that the user is getting the best ad. This is exactly how it should be!

There's a fun experiment I suggest my students do, which I invite you to try as well. I tell them to create two completely different thumbnails to test the same ad. I then get them to take the winning thumbnail, and write two different versions of the ad copy for their next attempt. Whichever copy is the winner, they take that copy and try the ad out with the winning thumbnail and a new one to test it against, and so on. If you try this yourself, you'll find the process never really ends because you keep trying to keep beating your last ad, with each one leveling up as you go.

So how do you know if your ads are working?

Here are five key things to look out for.

#1: Check your cost per click. With third world countries, you're looking at 0.1-0.3 cents per click at this time. For the USA and the other big four countries it's more like 0.5-0.11 cents per click. It could be even cheaper if the song and ad is really good.

#2: Check the ad itself to see if you're getting likes, comments or shares.

#3: This is the most important one. Are you seeing an increase in streams on your song, and / or an increase in followers? Is the song being added to any playlists? If people are resonating with your song then you should see a jump in all of these areas.

#4: If you're not getting the results you want, check the thumbnail: could you change it to something else more interesting or cool? You could also try testing a different part of the video, and looking at your call to action. Maybe the targeting is off?

#5: This is more advanced, but inside your ads manager look at performance and clicks and check the CTR. Your goal on Facebook should be 2% and up.

It's hard to know for sure why an ad isn't working out without seeing it, so if you find yourself in this position check out my Spotify 5-Day Challenge because I can give direct feedback there if needed. Join at **10xyourfanbase.com/livechallenge**.

Finally: Be patient

One mistake a lot of artists make is they turn off their ads too soon. They assume the ads aren't working, or they get overwhelmed, or they can't commit to seeing a campaign through. You need to give it time. In fact, don't even start Facebook or Instagram ads unless you are willing to commit to a 30-60 day campaign minimum. Again, I also highly recommend you choose one platform to get started with. Don't run ads on both Spotify and Facebook until you've mastered one first, otherwise you'll just burn a bunch of money because you haven't given it enough time and attention to make it work.

As we've noted, your goal with your Facebook ad is to trigger Spotify's algorithm by feeding it data. What we mean here is that Spotify is going to notice when more and more people are heading over there to listen to your songs, but you have to give it time to notice. And it will notice!

So please don't cut off your ad prematurely. Once Spotify realizes you're getting a good reaction, there's way more chance you'll get your song featured in those algorithmic playlists.

This is when things get exciting. You couldn't pay for what Spotify's algorithm can do for you.

As someone who's spent thousands on ads, I'm happy to say it only takes about $500-600 a month on a good performing Facebook ad campaign to trigger Spotify's algorithm for a song.

$500 a month works out to $16.6 per day. If you start with $5-10 and then scale up to $16 a day that's really doable and really worth it. YOU'RE worth it!

And my final point on Facebook ads is this one. It's more important, and a much wiser strategy, to run ads for the full 30-60 days spending a consistent budget of $16+ a day than spending the full $500 in just a few days. We don't just want a spike, but a continuous feed of streams going to Spotify so they can collect the data and get you on those playlists!

Chapter 12:
BEYOND SPOTIFY

As awesome as Spotify is, and as much as I love using it and teaching all the methods and strategies in this book, I have to say this. It's vitally important that we, as artists, stay as in control of our destiny as we can, and one of the ways we do that is by widening our horizons in the way in which we reach our fans.

Because what if we wake up tomorrow and Spotify has gone into liquidation and the platform folds? How do we stay in touch with those millions of followers that we've worked so hard to gain? Likewise there are no guarantees that Facebook, Instagram, Twitter, TikTok and YouTube will be around forever. Internet trends come and go, but the one thing, the one service that people have stayed with for the past two and a half decades is email.

And that's why, as we come to wrap this book up, I want to talk about the power of email marketing and why it's essential that you build an email list. I'll share tips and ideas that you can use to not only grow your email list, but also how to use email to communicate with your fans. And, of course, you can have links to your Spotify in any emails you send out, so it's all very connected and integrated. Let's take a look.

The power of email marketing

There's one big reason why I love communicating with my fans via email and it's this: it puts me in control. Once I have that very valuable piece of contact information, I can email or send messages out whenever I want and it'll land in a fan's inbox instantly. If I have a new song, or a tour, or a Crowdfunding campaign coming up I can promote it with the click of a button.

Spotify is awesome but as of yet it doesn't allow us to contact and follow up with our fans in the same way that emails do. And the truth is, more people buy songs, merch and show tickets via email than they do from ads we place on any platform.

How to do it

So how do we get that precious piece of information, the coveted email address?

Sure, you can do a regular post on social media linking to an opt-in page, and you can have a pop-up on your website that says something like: *Hey! Sign up for our email newsletter to keep up to date with releases, tour dates and more!*

And you might get a few people willing to give you their email address that way.

But it comes back to this question: What's in it for them?

And the answer is ... nothing much at all!

So... can you guess what I'm going to say?

Yep — you're going to give something away!

And what exactly are you going to give away?

Your best song(s) in exchange for an email address.

In fact, let's take it up a notch. To make this offer extra sexy, extra tempting and oh-so enticing — why not give away a full album? Honestly, if it gets you an email list with thousands of subscribers, it's worth it.

To reach the highest number of people, and to stand the best chance of getting those thousands of subscribers, I advise you to place an ad on Facebook offering a free download of a song — or a full album if you're feeling it.

You just need to create the ad so the link takes people to an opt-in page: a super-simple page where all they can do on this page is give you their name and email to get this awesome song or album for

FREE or leave. There are no other links or promotions to distract them. In fact the more simple the page, the better.

This is similar to what we looked at in Chapter Six. We're creating a download gate which allows people to claim your music. As a reminder, it's Distrokid that you want to use here. It will not only collect names and email addresses, but get them to pre-save your song on Spotify.

So before you create your ad, you're going to need to decide whether to use Distrokid and ClickFunnels if you haven't already. A regular website with something like Wordpress just isn't going to cut it here, they're way more limiting and just not designed for what we're going for. So please, go to https://smartmusicbusiness. com/freefunnel — that's my website, and that link will give you some templates you can use for free.

In terms of which email service to use, there are a few out there like MailChimp or Aweber, but personally I really like **Active Campaign** because it's super simple and affordable, plus the automation and tagging you can do within it is incredible. You can get a free trial **here**. If you like it and decide to use it, prices currently start at $9 per month for 500 subscribers. This is a small financial investment when you realize the sales and interest you can generate when you contact your fans in this direct and personal way.

So what about the first email that a new sign-up gets after they opt in for your free music? I'd say something like this:

Subject line: Your Music Downloads, or Free music from Manafest

Hey [first name] thanks for listening to my music, here's your free download — just click here.

Make sure 'click here' is hyperlinked. I usually use Dropbox to deliver my files.

Then go on to say:

Hope you love the music. Make sure you subscribe to my YouTube channel or follow me on Spotify.

This is also an opportunity to share something short and personal about how you got started in music, and why it means so much to you that they're listening to it.

Wherever you point them to, make sure it's the platform that you are most active on. Then sign off. It's that's simple! You can add a PS with a link to something you're selling, if you want, but be gentle with it at this early stage.

I have all these email addresses... now what?!

We don't want to build an email list just to have it sit there. All good email services allow you to set up automation (also known as a drip sequence), so that when someone joins your list they get a series of welcome emails automatically, and I recommend you use that feature.

For example, as well as the email I outlined above, have a sequence of emails set up to go out after someone has joined your list. Here's how I do it.

The first email is a welcome email and in there I share part of my story; essentially how I came to be a musician. My subject line is usually *Welcome To My World,* which gets a great open rate. Remember, if they don't open your email, they're not clicking on anything. It's too advanced for this book, but your goal with any email you send out should be that it gets opened, and generating curiosity in the subject line is the best way to encourage this.

At the end of this first email, I'll add a PS with a message like, *Make sure you check out my other albums or online store.* I'm very soft with the sell.

Over the next few emails I'll continue to share more stories about my journey in the music industry, and I'll also offer a coupon code which gives 20% off our entire store.

I like to space the emails out so that they're every day or every other day. I don't want to overwhelm my new fans, but I do want to stay in their awareness.

The key is to make these initial emails compelling. Share how you got started in music, or the story behind a song or music video. This is the time to get personal and bond with your fans so they feel like they know you.

After the initial welcome sequence, you probably want to be sending emails out a couple of times a week. You can write about new releases, your crowd funder, your tour. You can go as niche as you want in this, and be as personal as you feel happy with. You can include behind-the-scenes details or photos from a show you did, or even send photos of your pets, or just let your readers know how well your album is doing. Even if it's just a short email, include a call to action somewhere. If you're not promoting anything right now, you could link to a previous release on Spotify with a, *Hey, remember this?* nostalgia vibe.

In essence, be as creative and as sincere as you can. This is how you keep your fans interested and in the loop with what you're up to. Have fun and enjoy the fact that you can reach people in this way, and that you're in control. You own your email list, it's independent of any social platform, and, according to Forbes, the average expected ROI is $42 on every dollar you spend.

I don't know about you, but I find that pretty incredible!

Final thoughts

So we've reached the end of the book. How are you feeling? Motivated, inspired, and ready to carve an amazing career as an independent, trail-blazing, super-aware and creative artist on Spotify and beyond?

Good, that's what I've been going for!

Seriously my friend, I wish you all the good fortune in the world. I am confident when I say that you can have it all as a contemporary artist on Spotify if you're willing to try out the strategies and techniques on these pages. And if you need more support and inspiration, please join one of our monthly Spotify 5-Day Challenges at **10xyourfanbase.com/livechallenge.**

Here's a fraction of what you'll learn live. The most important aspect is that I get to speak to you personally so I can give you direct feedback about your music career.

Day 1 - 7 Alarming things you should know before you release a song on Spotify (#5 will blow your mind)

Day 2 - 3 hacks to triple your chances of getting on editorial and algorithmic playlists

Day 3 - Where to find collaborators to 10x your royalties and streams at no cost to you!

Day 4 - How to get 4x more followers using Spotify ads for profit!

Day 5 - The dirty truth about Spotify royalties and how to go to 6 figures without a record label

Way back at the start of this book I said I wanted to help you answer this question:

How do we get our music heard in such a crowded music marketplace?

And I've shared a lot of tried and tested ways you can do this, but the best marketing advice I can give you is this:

Have a great song.

And the best tool I believe you can take into the studio is a great song idea.

Songs are what drive the music business and without them the music economy would collapse.

So please, keep creating. If you keep creating AND you keep marketing, and never give up, your star will rise.

And I can't wait to see you soar.

Chris Greenwood, AKA Manafest

ADDITIONAL RESOURCES

Books by Chris Greenwood

From Red to Black: A Short Journey from Debt to Liberty

Fighter: 5 Keys To Conquering Fear & Reaching Your Dreams

How to Write and Release Your First Song: Songwriting Secrets from an Award-Winning Artist

Music Marketing Promotions Guide: Over 21 Tested and Proven Hollywood Marketing Strategies to Promote Every Song You Release

Music Business & Marketing Accelerator Using Instagram

The Truth About The Music Business: What Every Artist Needs To Know Before They Sign a Record Deal

Teach What You Know: A 12 Step Guide to Creating Your First Online Course & Earning Passive Income

YouTube Playbook for Artists & Musicians: Start Getting More Views, Comments, Royalties and Subscribers on Your YouTube Channel

Courses and Resources by Chris Greenwood

Spotify 5 Day Challenge:
https://www.10xyourfanbase.com/livechallenge

Smart Music Business:
https://www.smartmusicbusiness.com/

Smart Music Business Funnel Training:
https:// smartmusicbusiness.com/freefunnel

Spotify Ad Templates
https://www.smartmusicbusiness.com/spotifyadtemplates

Made in the USA
Columbia, SC
25 October 2024

45048485R00085